THE MAN AND HIS WORKS

St Patrick

The Man and His Works

Thomas O'Loughlin

First published in Great Britain in 1999

Society for Promoting Christian Knowledge
36 Causton Street
London SW1P 4ST
www.spckpublishing.co.uk

Reprinted once
Reissued 2014

British Library Cataloguing-in-Publication Data
A catalogue record for this book is available
from the British Library

ISBN 978-0-281-07213-2
eBook ISBN 978-0-281-07214-9

eBook by Graphicraft Limited, Hong Kong

Printed in Great Britain by Ashford Colour Press
Subsequently digitally printed in Great Britain

To the memory of my mother

REQUIESCAT IN PACE

NOTE

In several places in this book the biblical numbering does not correspond to that of a modern Bible. This is because Patrick used a text based on the Septuagint, and a numbering based on the Septuagint has been used here.

CONTENTS

One

THE ENIGMA OF *P*ATRICK

SOMEONE FOREIGN?

We all know about St Patrick, do we not? First of all, there is
the legend, in which he was the man who brought Christianity
single-handedly to Ireland. With this goes an image of big
bunches of shamrock and greenery. There are also umpteen tales
about him: he fought the Druids, he banished snakes, he was an
all-round mighty man. Next, there are the snippets of history.
Many people say he went to Ireland to bring Christianity in
AD 432, some say he died in 461, but others say it was 493. And
there are over a dozen places – from Devon and Somerset,
through Wales and the Severn valley all the way up to
Carlisle – that claim to be his birthplace. And new candidates
for this honour appear, on average, once every decade.

Then there are theories: there were two Patricks (aptly
named 'Patrick' and 'Old-Patrick'); one died in 461 and the
other in 493. He did not bring the ordinary Christianity of
the Roman Empire but a special kind of Christianity that is, as
it happens, far more user-friendly for today called 'Celtic
Christianity'. Another theory is that he was more a shaman than
a bishop, or that he was the last possessor of strange Druidic
powers. Lastly there is the saint: an apostle of Ireland, a patron,
an intercessor for the Irish, who bestows 'a sweet smile' 'on Erin's

green valleys', and the possessor of a liturgical feast on March 17. The list goes on and on: everyone with a religious drum to beat and any contact with Ireland or the fringes of Europe has lined him up as 'on their side'. And if not a full member of their group then he is at least a forerunner who would endorse their activities be they religious, political, military or some deadly combination of all three.

Here is the enigma of Patrick: he looms large on the imaginative horizon of so many people, yet he saw himself as a Christian bishop from the embattled edge of a crumbling empire. As such he is a man whose world, lifestyle and understanding are in many respects wholly foreign to us. With modern Christians he shares a faith – or, at least, both he and they recite the same creed. But many things taken for granted in his religious world hardly appear in the consciousness of Christians today; and many of the concerns of Christians today never crossed his mind.

Patrick was convinced that the universe was in its last days, that those who did not believe in Christ once they heard his name belonged to the party of the devil. He viewed the material creation as an arena where the divine was not only close, but constantly intervening. He lived in a world where demons are wicked creatures that dwell in the lower atmosphere and wander around doing wanton and wilful evil to the children of light. Angels too are everywhere. They behold the face of God, yet also dwell in the created universe; they can appear with messages, they can intervene with solace and power. All these interventions by non-material creatures are as nothing to the most perfect intervention and revelation of God: the first coming of the

Word made flesh. Through him all the secrets of the universe are laid bare; and from this vantage point of perfect knowing the Church preaches. Christ is still in the universe in his body, has imparted his power to that body, and Patrick as a bishop is one of those who wields that power. So we recite the same creed, but our expectations of how believing involves us in the whole structure of reality are radically different.

Likewise, Patrick would not understand modern religious concerns. He may be the saint of green valleys and green beer for his feast day, but he had no interest in ecology! On a more serious level, today Christians would consider slavery an evil opposed by both the gospel and natural human rights. Patrick knew slavery from the inside. Yet while he opposed the killing of Christian hostages, he never offers any criticism of slavery for, like St Paul writing to Philemon, it was just something in his world. The list of differences goes on and on.

READING PATRICK

Patrick has been the centre of a well-developed cult as a patron saint since sometime in the mid-seventh century. Since then he has been pressed into service in many ways as 'a national saint', a symbol more than a man. However, he has always attracted attention from the cult back to himself. In large part this can be explained as the natural interest in the man behind the legend, or because it is with Patrick that Ireland moved from prehistory (the time before which texts do not survive from a society) into history.

However, there is a wider appeal which has to do with the

fact that from Patrick's hand have come two, rather personal, documents. These draw to him people who are attracted neither to the cult nor to the earliest stratum of Irish history. Moreover, from the fifth century in the West we have no shortage of brief works in Latin by bishops – this was the period of the great flowering of theology in Gaul – but few of these works can boast a readership today to equal Patrick's. Both Patrick and those other bishops would have been shocked by this fact! But while the sermons of Caesarius of Arles and the wise instructions of Eucherius of Lyons bring us face to face with profound Christian learning, Patrick's works bring us a living human being. We read Patrick's two surviving documents and feel we are coming into contact with a real man of flesh and blood. We sense that he puts himself into his writings; we sense his hurts, angers, hopes and fears. Yet we also know that he lives in an alien place to us: it is neither the landscape of Ireland nor the landscape of Christianity (of whatever denominational variety) as we know it today. We sense the continuity and the foreignness. It is precisely this 'mixed feeling' of him being close to us and so very far away that makes his two short writings so valuable. Moreover, this value is not limited to those interested in religion in Ireland or the Celtic lands.

Reading these documents brings us face to face with a basic religious question: how can a religious document written in one culture and world of understanding be the bearer of a religious message that is larger than that culture? Can an account of human experience of the divine communicate that experience to someone who does not share the same understanding of the universe, the same frames of reference in scientific and religious belief, or the same cultural values? This is as true of the documents that make up the New Testament as it is true of Patrick, but Christians today have heard the Gospels so often that their foreignness is passed over, or we are so used to accommodating them into our view of reality that we do not notice that we hear them in a way very alien to that of the audience for whom they were first written. Patrick's documents are so short that we can get an overview of them in a way that we cannot with other longer texts such as one of the Gospels. In addition, they are unfamiliar and so pull us up sharply when they jar with our expectations about the Christian life or reality. Hence reading Patrick both fuels our interest in this curious figure, and raises basic questions of understanding and faith.

'THE PAST IS A FOREIGN COUNTRY'

Confronting texts from the foreign country of the past is both difficult and challenging. If we accept the possibility that we can make sense of documents from another culture and view of reality, then when we read them we are engaged in a complex act of translation, not just from Latin into English – a simple and straightforward technical matter – but from another culture and perception of reality into our own. This requires that we try to imagine how Patrick viewed reality – himself, life, others, the universe, and God – as we read his words. Only through this leap of imaginative sympathy can we hope to understand him. Only when we know his cultural language, his language-game, can we know what he wants to say. This cultural language is not

Latin, Late Latin, Vulgar Latin, nor any other systems of sounds, but his values, beliefs, and assumptions about what life is about, where it comes from, what it is for, and how people go about living and getting to that destination.

Learning a past language is difficult. A start is to learn from others who have made the past their special field of study; they can tell us about ancient social structures, fill in context, show how passages in Scripture were understood at a particular period, and explain what were the assumptions of Christians at that time about their religion. But trying to understand a writer is also an individual task: reading the words and seeking to imagine the sort of mind which that writer thought would be reading his words. For instance, Patrick would never have imagined that a woman would read his writings. So this task is neither simple nor swift, but it holds out the possibility that we meet the mind of the writer. The encounter is also unsettling; we see that many things that both our writer and we ourselves hold dear are relative. For instance, Patrick saw a direct link, based on his reading of the gospel, between his work at the very ends of the earth and Christ coming again 'to judge the living and the dead'. We have a different sense of space, a different way of reading Scripture, a different notion of the second coming, yet we may both be baptized and consider ourselves believers. The ancient text, in its very irrelevance to us, disturbs us.

Faced with this, one could pretend that cultures and human discoveries do not affect religious belief; one could escape to an imaginary world where we do not live in time as beings whose understanding is always partial. This world of 'eternal truths' and 'unchanging certainties' is the make-believe realm of fundamentalism. Another option would be to say that Christianity arose in that foreign past world and was part-and-parcel with that world; just as that world is gone, so its belief system is out of date. We are the successors of the past who must, if we are honest, jettison those beliefs that no longer fit with our understanding of the universe. But the world of modernity is as imaginary as that of fundamentalism. First, it assumes that we exist wholly independently of the past; and second, that we stand at the pinnacle of knowledge. Yet we are as much products of the past as of our own making. We inherit understandings, institutions and life itself. We exist in a culture in history. The past makes us, and we have to take that as a starting point. The past cannot be simply cut adrift. The past may be a foreign country but, to continue the metaphor, it is one with which we share a common border. We can only know the cultural language of our day by comparison with the past out of which it grew. Moreover, when it comes to matters of ultimate concern, each individual, each culture and each epoch is limited. Some aspects of the mystery of existence were clearer in the fifth century than today; some things clear to us were invisible to them. There is intellectual progress on the one hand, but the awareness that mystery is always beyond us on the other.

UNDERSTANDING IN TENSION

Confronting an ancient religious text which sincerely sets out its author's faith forces upon us the question of how we can say we share a faith with that author when we do not share the rest of the author's world. In the discovery of the writer's world we realize that all religious understanding exists within a set of tensions. There is the tension of past and present; neither is complete. There is a tension between our confidence in our understanding and our acknowledgement of our ignorance; we cannot opt for just one of these positions. There is the tension between speaking and silence. If we seek to express that which is beyond experience we betray the mystery in our reducing it to our culture; but we also betray that experience if, for fear of failure, we remain silent. These tensions are part of the basic tensions of faith. We are in this world and here we are called to live and love, to think and act; yet we see origins and ends beyond this world in the mystery of God.

Reading Patrick with this sense of tension turns a curious text from the last days of the Roman Empire in the West into an interesting adventure into what it is to know and believe. This is made all the more pointed as, in the process, we have to confront the difference between what we can actually find out about the historical Patrick and the image of Patrick that is conveyed in the legend. So we read this text with a triple agenda. First, we have to search out the man from the legend as best we can. The first task falls into the province of the historian and calls for critical detective work to set out what exactly we know of his life and times. Second, we have to extend our understanding to try to take in his world-view. This is the realm of the exegete, translating the foreign text into our world without compromising the integrity of either Patrick or ourselves. And third, we confront the questions of faith which are mysterious in every culture. This is the world of the theologian, asking if Patrick is a witness to a truth that is larger than any culture and its language. The first two tasks will be addressed in this introduction; the third cannot be addressed in a work whose primary aim is to present the text in translation. That is a task for the reader to take up, having read Patrick.

Reinventions of Patrick

Patrick is probably the best known fifth-century Christian in the world today. Theologians may argue that Augustine (354–430) was, and perhaps still is, more influential for how Christians present their beliefs, but how many New Yorkers parade on 28 August (his feast day)? However, the price of Patrick's popularity has been that he has been smothered by his legend and cult. Each age has adopted him, adapted him to a particular agenda, and remade him in its image. For example, in the seventh century Patrick was being used as the main plank in a campaign to establish the hegemony of the See of Armagh – that see's principal claim to primacy was that its bishops were the linear successors in the see Patrick had established. To this end they produced lives of the saint and lists of the places he visited. The message was clear: these were churches that had been established by him in his travels through the country and they now owed allegiance to his *coarb* (successor). By the time that the Book of Armagh was assembled (early eighth century), Patrick was not only the successful missionary, but was the one who determined the legitimacy of Irish centres of church authority and its policy towards the rest of Christendom.

Another medieval re-evaluation was that of Patrick as the wonder-worker of the Irish: his miracles and his intercession would save the people. As such he was seen to preside over all that was most noble in art, literature and society. He became Patrick, 'the national apostle'. This image was later developed as both 'national' and 'apostle'. Thus as the saint of the nation he stood for an independent country with a glorious past of gold and learning and saints. Pressed into this mould, the emphasis on St Patrick's Day in the latter part of the nineteenth century was an important feature in the development of an awareness of an Irish 'nation' as a culturally distinct entity. His day became the national holiday and 17 March takes its place with 4 July and 14 July. This should be balanced by earlier reuses of St Patrick in the service of the state, to which the now-ragged banners of the Knights of the Order of St Patrick in St Patrick's Cathedral, Dublin and the distribution of shamrock by their royal colonel-in-chief to the Irish Guards in London still bear witness.

Patrick as apostle also emerged from the realities of Ireland in the nineteenth century. As the Irish diaspora spread over the English-speaking world, they brought St Patrick as a character-istic element of the Catholicism that was often their only badge of proud identity. No one familiar with the dark probation to which the Irish emigrants were subjected can deny that Archbishop Hughes's decision in 1858 to name his cathedral in New York after Patrick – after facing down a decade of anti-Irish riots – gave these suffering people a well-earned pride. And similar, if smaller, buildings scattered across the English-speaking world remind us of the role of Patrick for a people who wanted to assert both their religion and, in muted way, their ethnic identity.

Patrick has also been employed by the theologians. In the aftermath of the Reformation his memory became disputed property. Was he in union with Rome or not? The affiliation of each writer seems always to have coincided with that of Patrick. Thus was his mission distinct from, or even in opposition to, that of Palladius sent by Pope Celestine? Was his 'Celtic Church' another distinct 'branch' of the ancient Church or was it 'one with Peter'? Both sides thought they could prove their credentials by having this fifth-century missionary on their side in a contest about sixteenth-century problems.

The need to re-evaluate has not subsided. On the one hand there is the view that he brought a killjoy religion with taboos about sex and pleasure to a fun-loving people. For others, he was exempt from this as was the 'Celtic Church' he founded (the killjoys came later with another 'institutional' Church that was guilt-ridden). Since we have so few documents from the period after him (what there are, are either obscure or show hardly any significant difference from the continental Church at the same time), there is little in the way of evidence to limit the scope of invention or the possibility of creating a 'Celtic spirituality' or 'Celtic Church' with whatever elements one would like to have in the Church today. Alas, the great surge of interest today in Christianity among those people who spoke Celtic languages runs the risk of smothering him again.

Letting Patrick Speak

If Patrick is to be heard we have to impose upon ourselves two strict disciplines. The first is to resist the natural desire to fill out the immediate background to Patrick with circumstantial evidence. We would all like to know when he lived, where he came from, what happened in his youth, and what he thought about a host of issues. But we know very little, and must be content with our ignorance. This is frustrating and against our instincts, so we should acknowledge that the desire to fill in gaps with speculation is a powerful one. We may laugh at some of the imaginary fillers invented by medieval hagiographers, but we are not automatically immune.

Second, we must try to see the text against its background, not as a preparation for us and our background. Patrick was a citizen of the Roman Empire, a bishop of the catholic Church, a provincial, and someone caught up in the politics of bishops and warlords in the fifth century. He was not someone seeking to reconstruct a spiritual vision in the face of the problems of modern life and our religious questions. He is not an example to be copied, nor an object lesson, nor some kind of teacher of wisdom. He is a voice from the distant past whose distinctiveness we should respect.

So is there any value in reading him today? Christianity is a religion of history. It traces its roots into the history of the people of Israel; it sees its centre in the coming in history of the Christ; it sees itself straining forward in history towards an end. In such a faith, looking backwards to the past is not equivalent to making a trip to a museum, but is more like the people of a village continually returning to a well. Seeing how earlier Christians, in very different circumstances, faced the trials of discipleship is part of a process of problem solving for our lives today. Shifting our gaze from looking solely at our own problems, ideas and theology to the past is a form of lateral thinking. Knowing how someone solved a different problem in a different situation can spark off ideas in our minds, give us fresh perspectives, help us to make connections we had not thought of before.

Reading the past while respecting its difference is the opposite to ransacking the past as evidence for our concerns or precedents for our positions. The reader wishes to visit and learn how things were done differently, and the unfamiliar is the surprising; the ransacker already knows what they are looking for, and the unfamiliar is the rubble to be cleared away. The first path, especially with an awkward text like Patrick, is not only more difficult, but does not bring the political advantages of bringing a famous name to the support of a cause. However, it is probably a more honest approach to reality.

Two

℘ATRICK: LIFE AND TIMES

This chapter title is deliberately provocative. For centuries to discover the life and times of Patrick has been the aim of hagiographers and historians, but in all likelihood no such chapter can be written. The fifth century – generally agreed to be when Patrick lived – is a dark age in our knowledge of the history of Roman Britain, and our knowledge of Ireland is just beginning to shift from what we can learn from the archaeology of a non-literate society to a history derived from documents. Indeed, the situation regarding evidence is extreme: we have Patrick's writings, one other detail, and a scholarly backdrop provided by archaeology. But while we bemoan this lack of information about Patrick, we must note that we still know more about him than any other individual or event in the insular world at the time.

This position is in sharp contrast to the amount of information that can be found in books about Patrick from prior to 1962 when an essay by D. A. Binchy ushered in a new era in studies of Patrick, but this ignorance represents a desire to separate what we can verify from contemporary sources from guesswork hallowed by age and repetition. So we are thrown back on what we can learn from the *Confessio* and the *Epistola*. Unfortunately, neither contains a time reference that allows us to fix any date with accuracy, and the few places that are named can no longer be identified. Let us deal with these questions first.

DATES

The most common date linked with Patrick is that he arrived in Ireland on his mission in 432. Indeed, it has a hallowed status as the symbolic date for the beginning of written history in Ireland. The association of the date with Patrick goes back at least as far as one of his early hagiographers, Muirchú, writing in the late-seventh century. I shall avoid describing Muirchú as a 'biographer' as this brings to mind the notion of seeking to understand a life. The hagiographer has a specific agenda relating to the promotion of someone already recognized as a saint: the focus is on the person-become-saint and who is active now, rather than the man or woman as fellow humans (see Delehaye, 1998).

The link of 432 with Patrick occurred in this way. The fifth-century Gaulish writer, Prosper of Aquitaine (*c*.390–*c*.463) compiled a *Chronicle* which listed important events in history against the date of their occurrence. For the period before his own time he simply copied earlier lists of notable dates, but for the period of the second quarter of the fifth century (425–55) he used his own knowledge and is reliable. Against the year 431 he records this fact without any elaborative comment: 'Palladius, ordained by Pope Celestine, was sent to the Irish who are believers in Christ as their first bishop.' What prompted this action, who Palladius was, and what happened to him are all unknown. This sentence in Prosper is the one occasion that Palladius appears on the radar screen of history.

Wholly distinct from this piece of evidence is the reality of Patrick and his mission. It is certain that he was in Ireland preaching the gospel, and from his writings we are told that he went not to believers but pagans, and indeed he went where no Christian had hitherto gone. Now arises a problem: these distinct bits of evidence do not dovetail together, and could even be construed as contradictory. Who was first? Who did the work of converting? One cannot deny Patrick's claims (particularly if one holds him as one's patron saint) and one cannot deny the fact behind Prosper's entry (and for all the medievals, and some of the moderns, who looked at this problem there was the additional desire not to seem to slight 'the apostolic authority' of being sent by the pope).

The first writer we know of who recognized the problem was Muirchú who thought up a rather clever solution that saved all the details. Ireland's first bishop was Palladius who was sent from Rome, where he had been the pope's archdeacon. But when he and his companions got to Ireland they found it a hard and cold mission, and decided to return home. Palladius reached Britain on his return journey, but then died. The way was now open for the missionary, chosen by heaven, to step into the gap: Patrick. So the date 432 entered Irish history; its rationale being that Patrick had to arrive after 431, but so soon after as to ensure that no appreciable conversion could have occurred (as that would take from Patrick's authority as head of the whole Irish Church).

Now to the date of Patrick's death: is it 461 or 493? The answer is that we do not know. Both these dates are found in Irish annals, and if we were to assume that they are utterly reliable sources for historical dating (as many until the mid-twentieth century did) then we would have a problem. In fact, a chronicle can be trusted in so far as it records contemporary events directly (for example, Prosper for 431) or draws on a source that itself was a contemporary record (for example, Prosper draws upon Eusebius/Jerome whose chronicles are accurate for the late-third and fourth centuries). Using that criterion, the Irish annals are accurate from about the mid-seventh centuries onwards. However, most chronicles contain far more than contemporary evidence and are, in fact, universal histories situating events within a pattern of world history that runs in ages from the creation to the present. The Irish annals are no exception to this and so 'record' many events both in world history and the history of Ireland that long pre-date actual record-keeping. They knew from Prosper of the date of 431; they used the logic found in Muirchú, or drew directly from him, for 342; but also knew that Patrick had to have a date of death. This latter date was indeed of great importance, for the date of a saint's death was seen as their date of birth in heaven. Then by some creative calculation or by relying on some tradition about Patrick's age when he died, they added that figure to 432 and got their various answers. In short, the annals neither individually nor collectively can be trusted for any date in the fifth century.

On one point about Patrick's death there is agreement: that is that it took place on 17 March, and hence his feast day. This date is found in several early liturgical calendars (for example, that of Willibrord from the early eighth century). Although these written sources are later, since one of the most stable elements in any tradition regarding a saint is the day of death, we should not discount them as evidence. Thus there is good reason to assume that this date for his day of death preserves an authentic detail from the immediate circle of Patrick.

One other date keeps cropping up with reference to Patrick: that he made his escape from slavery in Ireland, aged twenty-two, sometime shortly after 407–10. His age at the time of his escape is based on details supplied in the *Confessio*, but that it was shortly after 407–10 (a date that also fits with 432) is based on a brilliant bit of guesswork by J. B. Bury (1905). The basis of this is that Patrick says he was on board ship for three days, and then he wandered through 'a desert' for twenty-eight days. Bury suggested that a three-day voyage would exclude Britain, so he must have taken a ship to Gaul. But how could Gaul be a desert when it was the source of wine, theology and good Latin? Well, it had been devastated in the great barbarian invasion of 407–10 and Patrick's desert was a trip through a war zone in the aftermath of the enemy (see Bury, 1905, pp. 338–42).

This suggestion is ingenious, but it tries to prove too much and begs too many questions. The three-day voyage is too vague: is it seventy-two hours or an evening, a day, and a morning (note the parallel with Christ's three days in the tomb)? How far do you sail in three days, anyway, when we do not know where he left from, the wind conditions, and the quality of the seamanship? As to the reference to the desert, it seems more like a spiritual theme rather than an itinerary. The theory's elegance, its ability to explain a troublesome episode in the *Confessio*, linked to the satisfaction of having a date of birth for Patrick

(385–8), can make it intoxicating. But its evidence base is very narrow, and demands that we can take every detail in Patrick as accurate and exact (a demand we make of few works written many years later and relying on memory), and then accept a range of unverifiable assumptions about transport, navigation, and the possible cause of the situation described by Patrick. For a handy critique of Bury, see J. F. Kelly, 1985; for a new version of the theory – but one which falls into the same trap – see R. Keogh, 1997.

PLACES AND PEOPLE

Patrick mentioned five places: Ireland, Britain, Gaul, Bannavem Taburniae, and 'wood of Foclut near the western sea'. It is the last two that attract interest, but all we can say with certainty is that the first was in Britain, the other in Ireland. It would be a tedious task to list all the attempts that have been made to identify these places, but none of these attempts amounts to anything more than guesswork. Sometimes the attempts use dubious bits of military folklore, sometimes intricate arithmetic, and sometimes similarities of sound between these names and modern place names.

The place-name theories are not convincing over such a time-span due to changes in language and the fact that we are not sure what Patrick actually wrote in the *Confessio*, for the manuscripts vary as do modern scholars' opinions about the form of the name. Recently, for example, David Howlett (1994) has argued that one place name should be 'Banneventa Burniae'. Likewise, arguments about distances suppose that Patrick kept a modern map of Ireland in his pocket, so trying (outside the Roman Empire) to work backwards from mileages mentioned in texts where you do not know the location of both point A and point B is like asking the length of a piece of string.

My own favourite theory is a military one expounded by a friend some time ago. It runs like this: Patrick was captured during 'an amphibious raiding operation'. Such raids require 'assault craft' and 'landing areas' for such craft. They would not be able to carry horses on these, so the raiders had to be infantry. These could only 'operate' within a day's radius of 'the landing area' as they would have to get back on board before a cavalry 'counter-offensive' could be launched, and so on. In short, when cliffs and other bits of hostile coastline are removed from the equation, there are only so many places on the western coast of Britain where Patrick could have been captured. Well, it is a good story, but no more than saying that since he was captured by raiders, then he had to have been where the raiders could actually raid! In the final analysis, we have the fact that over 1,300 years ago, Muirchú no longer knew where these places were and engaged in guesswork. If their exact locations were then already lost, our chances – unless we find something like an inscribed stone – are next to zero.

Patrick also mentions the names of people: his father and grandfather, and the wicked Coroticus. His family are not known apart from his writings, while attempts to identify Coroticus usually turn on guessing what sort of Celtic name would sound like 'coroticus' in Latin. And however we construe that name, we have no independent evidence about such a ruler.

SKETCHING IN PATRICK'S
BACKGROUND

Patrick was born on the island of Britain: there his parents lived, there was his home, there was the place he missed so much. But while this was his 'own place', it is neither an ethnic nor political description. Patrick was politically a citizen of the Roman empire, and during the whole of his life – let us assume he died before 476 – there was a Western emperor in Rome. He is proud of this Roman heritage for he tells us that his father was a *decurion* (clergy-class, *Epistola* 10) which implied he belonged to the long-suffering, overtaxed rural gentry of the provinces. These were the class that bore the labour of maintaining a Roman presence in the countryside far from Rome. They paid the taxes and expected Rome's civil life and protection, namely the legions, in return. By the fifth century theirs was a forlorn hope. They still struggled to keep the Roman presence, but the legions were withdrawn, and they were left to their own devices to protect themselves from bandits and raiders. Patrick's case brings this out very well: he is proud of his social standing, and of Rome. Yet the protection of Rome was not there to save him from being captured and taken into slavery.

So was he Welsh, British or English? Well, he was not English; the invasions of the Angles, the Saxons and several other groups were still in the future. Moreover, 'Welsh' only becomes a significant term when it stands for the population of Britain apart from the Germanic invaders. So did he belong to the ethnic population of the island, the British, who had become romanized? It is quite possible, and some scholars have advanced the notion that his spoken language was akin to Old Welsh on the basis of some phrases that are reported from him and which were not intelligible to the reporters. More work needs to be done on this, but in the end it makes little difference, for Patrick's conscious identification is not in doubt.

PATRICK'S CHRISTIANITY

Patrick's family pride was not limited to their civil position but included their status in the Church, for he came from what amounts to a clerical dynasty: his father was a deacon and his grandfather a priest. Therefore Christianity was deeply embedded in his background. This raises the question as to what he meant by saying that he 'did not yet know the true God' when he was taken to Ireland. However, he knew enough about God to pray and to seek deliverance. This is probably explained by the practice of baptism not taking place until late in life.

Children were brought up within a Christian context but were not actually baptized until they had expressed their own desire to put the 'old lives' behind them; then when they were ready for Christian commitment, baptism washed away all their sins up to that point. This delaying of baptism, sometimes until the last possible moment, was not so much a statement about the nature of baptism as about the possibility of having sins forgiven. Baptism removed sins committed up to then, but what if a Christian committed serious sins (murder, fornication, and apostasy being those always mentioned) after baptism? Could these be forgiven? The reply was that they could be forgiven but only through a very laborious process, and then there was only one such chance offered to the sinner. To be baptized in this context was to make a very serious commitment indeed, and practical wisdom became 'sow one's wild oats, and then have the whole slate cleared by baptism' – a practice which effectively destroyed the sacramental life of Christians. Moreover, it was only in the early fifth century that Augustine began to point out the necessity of baptism for infants lest they die and not enjoy heaven. While this became a very distorted theory later on, it was probably prompted initially by the desire to combat the rather mercantile notion of God's mercy involved in the practice of 'sin now, baptism later'.

It is this notion of baptism that was probably operative in Patrick's household; he would hear about Christ from his parents, but truly coming 'to know God' (that is, being joined into Christ's life in baptism) could come later.

In so far as we can reconstruct Patrick's system of beliefs there is nothing that distinguishes him from the average Western bishop at the time. Where he models part of his *Confessio* around the creed, he does so with the same care not to fall into heresy regarding either the doctrine of the Trinity or the doctrine of Christ that is found among all orthodox Christian writers at the time. His understanding of the relationship of Christ to the community of his followers (the Church), again follows the standard Western pattern of seeing the Christians and Christ not as a collection of individuals meeting another individual (Jesus Christ), but rather as forming a corporate entity (Jesus as the head and each Christian being a different bit – member – of this vast body).

Likewise with regard to the interaction of Christ and each member (the theology of grace) Patrick takes a standard Western view which was far more balanced than the extreme position expounded by Augustine against Pelagius. Augustine had stressed the impotence of Christians in their salvation – it was solely God's grace that brought humanity back into the divine domain. Most theologians recognized that there had to be a human element: a desire to be a disciple and constant effort. Moreover, if human dignity was to have any meaning, then those efforts had really to contribute to the relationship with God. They therefore bowed to the great Augustine, but pointed out to people the importance of their work and discipleship, by which they collaborated with grace. It was neither God simply pulling them up, nor they climbing up themselves, but a process that involved both God and the human being in a mysterious 'assisted climb'. Those who continued to expound this sensible approach in the aftermath of Augustine were eventually smeared with the label 'semi-Pelagian' for their troubles; and the theological to and fro over this issue has dragged on ever since. Patrick was probably aware of these debates, but it is unlikely that he was consciously reflecting them in his thought. The simple fact is that if one is going out to preach conversion and discipleship, one has to have a working theology that includes an understanding of the value of human effort.

However, if Patrick's understanding of the content of Christian faith is not distinctive, his perception of how the divine plan for the universe impacts on him and includes him – what we might call his 'spirituality' – is highly personal. He is the chosen vessel to bring the gospel to the last place on earth, and so the herald of the last times. This theme is explored a little further in the next chapter of this introduction.

EDUCATION

One area that has attracted much comment over the years is the quality of Patrick's education or, as the question is more usually phrased: What is the quality of his Latin? The judgement usually comes out against him. However, while Patrick states that he did not have the opportunity to become someone with literary polish, we should not accept the negative judgement without comment. First, against what standard is ability in Latin judged? Older scholars had an ideal 'classical' language in mind and marked him down as if he were an undergraduate reading classics. This is certainly the wrong approach: the 'classical' language is a grammarian's ideal as derived from a very restricted canon of great writers – all several centuries before Patrick and who wrote with a deliberate interest in style and literary elegance. The actual language of everyday life was certainly very different, but does not survive. Moreover, the written language was not frozen: we see this in the language of the theologians of the fifth century who, by classicists' standards, wrote a far rougher or more rugged language.

Moreover, even these writings are the product of people who saw themselves as writers and were therefore consciously literary. But there is a great difference between two literate speakers of any language, say English, one of whom has the writing of texts as part of their livelihood, and one who only occasionally has to write anything longer than a note. Documents produced by this second group (people who would not describe themselves as 'writers' but who sometimes have to write) tend to be ephemeral, and if they survive it is only by accident. Patrick belongs to this group.

We have very few such documents from the period of Patrick – and nothing similar from anyone we can put into his circle in either Britain or Gaul. So all comparisons are flawed. The nearest document for comparison is the account of the Holy Places by Egeria written in *c.*384. Like Patrick she was writing because an occasion gave rise to it, rather than as part of her professional work. And, interestingly, she too has both his immediacy and has had the quality of her Latin damned by modern scholars.

I suspect we should approach Patrick with a different frame of reference. First, the state of Latin as a living vehicle of communication in Britain at the time is an unknown; consequently we cannot make meaningful comparisons and certainly not against some notional standard. Second, we should view him as a bishop occasioned to write, rather than as a literary figure; consequently we should ask how effectively did he get his message across to his reader. Third, while undoubtedly he did not have a 'smooth run' in education, we should balance any allowance made for this by the possibility that he is just invoking humility.

More recently a new attitude to Patrick's abilities has been making headway in the wake of David Howlett's 1994 study of complex numerical patterns and symmetries built into Patrick's prose. Howlett advances a most intriguing – and attractive – case, but it is one that raises as many questions as it solves. Can we be sure these patterns were in the mind of Patrick? How could he have learned such techniques? Can we be sure of the method with such a small evidence sample? and so on. This is not to dismiss Howlett's argument, but merely to point out that there is much work to be done before we judge one way or the other. For now, Howlett is not a solution, but a proposition to be assessed.

There is another way, however, to assess Patrick's skill which is to see the subtlety with which he used the one source he openly acknowledged: the Scriptures. This is not the place to advance the argument; rather I wish simply to set it out for your own judgement. When asked to produce a new translation of Patrick, the one prospect that encouraged me to take on the task (for there are so many in existence) was that it would offer an opportunity to gather together all the additional scriptural references I have made over the years in the margins of my copies of White (1905) and Bieler (1952). Once I had then set about the work, I discovered many more, so that the biblical apparatus in this translation is larger than that in any previous study – Conneely (1993) being the closest in quantity of references.

When one notes how carefully Patrick assembles biblical quotes and precedents into a mosaic to drive forward his argument, one is left with the impression of someone with great powers of attention and argument. This skill is not that of the proverbial 'man of one book' who can cite Scripture at every turn, for he draws together passages using a particular exegesis of each; then when these are linked together a new theological insight emerges. In any case, the references are given in italics in the text. Follow them out yourself, and then form a judgement.

Since the question of education has so often been reduced to the question of ability with Latin, this is a fitting place to mention Patrick's knowledge of languages. That Patrick could communicate in Latin is certain, but what of other languages? The vernacular languages of the British islands at the time were all members of the family of languages we now call 'Celtic'. However, these languages break into two subfamilies, one known as 'Q-Celtic' (the modern languages of Irish, Manx and Gallic) and the other 'P-Celtic' (the modern languages of Welsh, Cornish and Breton). At the time of Patrick it was earlier forms of these languages that were spoken. In Ireland the language was that which now is called 'Old Irish', while over most of the island of Britain it was the language now called 'British' or 'Old Welsh' – the direct forebear of modern Welsh.

Moreover, just as P-Celtic and Q-Celtic are now mutually unintelligible, so they were unintelligible then. And we should note that the people of the fifth century did not have our tools of comparative language study, so they would not have recognized these languages as related. An Irish raider in Wales in the fifth century would not have understood the local inhabitants, nor vice versa, and would have had no fellow feeling on the basis of being 'fellow Celts'. The two languages were for them as foreign as any two languages could be.

So did Patrick speak these languages? Well, he certainly spoke Irish or he would not have been able to communicate with all but a handful of people who were engaged in trade with the Roman world. It is most probably that he also spoke British (it would be slightly anachronistic to call it Welsh at this time). Not only would this have been the language of the countryside where he grew up, but certain curses are attributed to Patrick in later hagiography which could be explained on the basis that the words (meaningless to the later writer) were originally British.

It might seem to break the rules of evidence used above to invoke these later lives at this point; however, this exception follows a well-known pattern. Often phrases that are held to have power in themselves (usually curses) are transmitted as an exact sound rather than in translation. The best example is 'Raka' in Matthew 5.22 which was retained in the text as it was held the actual sound was what was sinful rather than the idea behind it. And, just as such survivals in the Gospels which were meaningless to the audience of the text are indicators of words going right back to Jesus, so such survivals in later 'lives' point to an actual recollection of a sound uttered by Patrick. So we can say that Patrick was certainly bilingual, and most probably trilingual.

IRELAND AT THE TIME

We think of the Roman empire as a great urban system linked by language, laws, roads, institutions, a taxation and postal service, a fairly uniform pattern of administrative units, and guarded by the legions. This image is so powerful that we unconsciously imagine that those on its edges had none of these things and were rough and ready primitives. However, while the pattern of social organization was very different, this does not mean that these were not highly sophisticated societies. It is no longer fashionable to say that 'outside the empire lived barbarians/ savages'; but this does not mean that we are free of the attitude. Moreover, we often transform rather than reject the picture of 'the primitive' and 'the savage'. They become 'noble savages' or 'people in touch with the primal realities'.

But such images, positive and negative, are untrue to the facts. What we know of early Irish society shows it to be a sophisticated and confident culture that was capable of holding itself culturally, as well as militarily, distinct from Rome. This picture is built up from a mixture of contemporary archaeological evidence, for it appears that literacy came in the wake of Christianity, and later written Irish sources. These written sources show a society with an elaborate system of law and custom which could not have emerged overnight and so we assume that at least the major elements of that social organization were there in the fifth century.

If you wish to get a better grasp of the society in all its details there is no better route than to read Fergus Kelly's book on early Irish farming (1997). There he traces the evidence for farm organization, food production, who did what on the farm, what animals were kept, and how exchange of goods and services took place using the twin tracks of archaeology and early Irish law. These sources used in conjunction reveal in close-up the society and life of the people with whom Patrick lived.

A simpler way of gauging that society is to look at some of the decorative metalwork that was produced and reflect on the artistic and metallurgical skills that are needed to make such items. Then reflect on the social organization that must be there to support that industry; not only wealthy patrons and a stable working environment, but trade links, communications and methods of exchange. Whether one reads Kelly or reflects on what is needed before one can make the Tara brooch, one quickly sees that descriptions of 'primitive warrior elites' – noble or ignoble – must be wide of the mark.

RELIGION IN IRELAND BEFORE PATRICK

One of the most complex questions discussed in relation to Patrick concerns the extent to which there were Christians in Ireland before Patrick's time. That there were such Christians is one of the few facts about the period we know independently of Patrick. Prior to 431 there were some Irish who were believers, for it is to that group that Pope Celestine sent Palladius. Moreover, since we have abundant evidence of trading links with the Roman empire – and even of a Roman trading post in Ireland – it is inconceivable that Ireland would have been untouched by Christianity. Unfortunately, the extent of the Christian presence in Ireland cannot be quantified.

So what was the extent of Patrick's mission? For the later hagiographers anxious to show the dependence of the whole Irish Church on Patrick's 'successor' in Armagh – and indeed that he had a link with Armagh is itself unprovable unless we argue in circle – there was no part of Ireland that was not converted by him or his direct disciples. However, even if Ireland is a small island, it is still a big mission field for one man – even with a team of disciples. Again, the answer is that we do not know; but

Patrick is still the only missionary whom we actually know anything about!

Regarding the religious situation in Ireland prior to Patrick among those who were non-Christians, there has been much speculation in recent years – often a picturesque mixture of wishful thinking and the jargon of the New Age movement – but, again, the answer is that we do not know. In the absence of writings by Irish non-Christians themselves, we have three possible sources of information: archaeology; what Roman non-Christians wrote about the religion of the Celts (usually in Gaul several centuries earlier); and what later Christians wrote about their pagan ancestors. All three sources are limited, and even together tell us very little.

Archaeology can point out ritual sites and objects belonging to the cult, but these discoveries are mute; they do not tell us what constituted the content of belief. A burial site may point to a belief in the afterlife – but that is hardly specific. Was there a heaven or a parallel world or a cycle of rebirths? Likewise, what we take to be a sacred enclosure may indicate worship, but were they monotheists or polytheists? Should one say they were 'sun-worshippers' when the image of the sun is used in so many religious systems – and some of those that use it, such as Christianity, would reject the notion of sun-worship entirely.

References to Celtic religion by classical authors would seem to be an ideal window into contemporary religious thought, but these have to be approached with care. First, they were observations made from the 'outside' of that system, and often were made according to an existing model of what a religion should be. Thus, the famous comments of Posidonius (see Tierney, 1959) on the religion of the Gauls tells us as much about a Stoic's view of what any religion is (or should be), as it does about what the Gauls actually thought. Second, these insights are partial, fragmentary, made by members of a victorious culture, and concern a culture several centuries earlier with which the Irish, even of that time, would probably have recognized no kinship. The Pan-Celtic world is only known to those who read the reports of archaeologists and the studies of philologists.

The reports of later Christian writers, such as Muirchú, also have to be read with caution. Not, as had become a common-place in popular writing, because he was 'a Christian who would have it in for the pagans', but because he saw all religions as forming part of a pattern leading up to Christianity. Muirchú – and virtually every other medieval theologian – did not view the relation of Christians and pagans using a binary view of Christians/Pagans; true/false; good/bad; saved/damned (that is, Christianity is true, good, and leading to salvation, while pagan-ism is false, evil and leading to damnation). This simple black-and-white theology only comes into the picture in the sixteenth century. Muirchú saw the relationship as one of preparation and fulfilment based on the model of Paul's speech in Athens (Acts 17.22–31). This was combined with Paul's references to a 'natural knowledge' of God's existence and power in Romans 1 and 2. Taken together these form a view of paganism as a deviation from the truth, but which has many true elements upon which Christianity can come and build. It is a model of incompleteness and perfection.

Thus pagan society and worship is a preparation for the gospel, and indeed can know itself to be incomplete without the gospel. When the gospel comes it brings complete answers and the perfect worship. This theory – blatantly at work in Muirchú and just beneath the surface in Patrick's attitude to preaching the gospel – disposed medieval Christians to record those elements of earlier religions which they perceived as definite pointers towards the 'fulfilment' of Christianity.

An incidental consequence of that Christian view is that they did not see aspects of the earlier religion which continued to exist in Christian times as 'pagan survivals' (such 'survivals' are seen only within the post-sixteenth-century perspective where they are equivalent to impurities in Christianity) but simply as part of 'the law of nature' (that is, bits of true religion apart from the gospel) that were not abrogated, but given a perfect direction in the 'law of the Scriptures'.

When we consider these limitations on the three sources of information about pre-Christian religion we are left in a position where the best course is caution regarding details. Lack of information is always tantalizing, the desire to know always drags us forward; but succumbing to that desire in the absence of good evidence does not remove ignorance, but adds to it.

— Three —

$\mathcal{P}$ATRICK'S WORLD

How do I see myself in space and time? This is not the sort of question we often ask ourselves consciously. Indeed, when space and time are thought of at all it is usually as sets of impersonal coordinates forming a grid relating locations and events: an entry 'meeting, room x' against a line in a diary. However, if we want to get inside the world of someone who comes from a culture different from our own, such as Patrick, these are very valuable questions.

Quite apart from grids of time and space that are external to us, we live in another space and time which is personal. This sense of time and place, of its nature, is not public even when it is shared by many in a community or society. It is our private sense of where we are now and of how far away some events or places are from us. While some events took place 'long ago' and are almost forgotten, others – an equal number of years ago – are 'pivotal' and still important to us. We think of certain places as our own or 'familiar', but other places as distant, strange, even alien. These personal notions of space and time are very hard to tie down. Often we are barely conscious of them and we only externalize them, in ways that others can glimpse, incidentally. These attitudes usually remain vague, just beneath our horizon of consciousness.

For reconstructing an individual's sense of space and time we need personal documents, and especially autobiographical materials. Here is the great irony regarding Patrick: while we have almost no fixed dates or locations, the sources do contain many clues as to his personal sense of time and place. His *Confessio* is clearly autobiographical, and the *Epistola* only slightly less so in that Patrick is a central actor in the events surrounding it. So, on the one hand, the information that is usually the easiest to obtain about dates and places is here beyond reach; but, on the other hand, that which eludes us in so many medieval sources is in Patrick's case readily at hand.

A STRANGER

The most obvious clue to how Patrick saw his location is that it is 'among strangers'. Repeatedly he declares that he is away from home and an alien in Ireland. This sense of being apart appears as something quite acute: he does not belong to this place or its people, and his home is not just across the sea in Britain (*Confessio* 23) but it is far away. The *Confessio* opens with a statement of where home is: Bannavem Taburniae. This is a place he knows well and identifies with. His family have deep roots there as members of the *decurion*/clergy-class, and he expects the reader likewise to know it (*Confessio* 1). Taken from home he suffers the consequences of not studying his own language and of having to express himself in an alien tongue (*Confessio* 9). But this suffering is justified by its end: for he has been, and is, prepared 'to hear the hatred of wanderer' (Sirach

29.30) in order that he preach the gospel (Mark 13.10) to the Irish (*Confessio* 37).

This juxtaposition of scriptural texts, Sirach and Mark, is interesting for understanding Patrick as a 'foreigner for the gospel'. Sirach 29.28–35 sets out the primary needs of a man for life and happiness. Basic to a happy life is living in one's own home with one's own family. Sirach asks, 'What are a man's first needs?' and replies that they are, 'Water, bread, clothing, and the safety of a home.' Indeed, the poor man with a home is better than one living in the presence of splendour without one. The little man dwelling in his own home is far better off than the stranger wandering from house to house accepting hospitality. It is a bitter thing to be homeless and it invites one to be reviled. As long as you are with your own people and in your home you do not have to hear the hatred that is heaped on the stranger. Sirach captures the sense of alienation felt by so many who have had to live as exiles or immigrants in a society which does not welcome them, and at the same time promotes the notion of home found in the rhyme: 'Be it ever so humble there's no place like home.' This whole passage from Sirach, not just the line Patrick quotes, seems to capture his sense of being a stranger where he is.

When, moreover, Sirach is read in combination with the statements of Christ on preaching from Mark, Patrick's self-portrait seems complete. In Mark the preacher of the gospel has to abandon home, brothers, sisters, mother, fathers, children and his own fields (Mark 10.29); he suffers insults and is dragged before his own religious leaders in the synagogues and before kings and rulers where he has to bear witness to Christ (Mark 13.9–10). So for Patrick to be a preacher is to be cut off from home and family, to have the lot of the suspect stranger, and to suffer the extremes of homesickness for he has no home in Ireland. In *Confessio* 37, Patrick's presentation of his experience seems to fit with this reading of the Scriptures down to the last detail. Grace (here presented as equivalent to the divine will), not himself, sent him to Ireland to preach, so he lives among strangers, endures insults from aliens (unbelievers), is taunted as a foreigner, treated as a prisoner, hears hatred uttered against him, and endures many persecutions.

But this theme of suffering as a stranger is a recurring one. He repeatedly notes that he has left his parents (*Confessio* 23, 43; *Epistola* 1), those he would like to have as friends (*Confessio* 43), and his homeland (*Confessio* 43; *Epistola* 1) for the sake of the gospel. Indeed, he has given up his own estate for his mission (*Confessio* 1) which echoes those in Mark 10 who have given up their own fields for the gospel. He has been held in contempt (*Confessio* 1), has had to forage for food (*Confessio* 22) and been despised (*Epistola* 1); these are the dangers Sirach sees facing the foreigner. He has been betrayed by those close to him (*Confessio* 32), had plots hatched against him (*Confessio* 35), has been brought before his own religious leaders and rejected (*Confessio* 26–7, 29), and brought before foreign kings (*Confessio* 52) and judges (*Confessio* 53). All these problems are consistent with what is foretold in Mark 13 for the preacher. And having been taken, in his youth, as a captive to an alien land, he takes up again that slavery – and with it exile – in response to a divine call (*Confessio* 37, 43, 61; *Epistola* 10). The gospel's task alone, he tells us, explains his spending his life far from home and family (*Confessio* 61), for as a young man he was told to go home from there (*Confessio* 17) and later told to go back to preach (that is, leave home) (*Confessio* 23).

Implicit in these directions is that Ireland is an alien place and that Patrick dwells there among 'the nations' (*Confessio* 48). In the *Epistola* (11) this experience of being without his home is presented as a basic quality of ministry founded directly on the teaching and experience of Christ: 'a prophet has no honour in his own land' (John 4.44). While he quotes John, he has in mind an image of this text that is based on all the uses of this theme in the Gospels (cf. Matthew 13.57; Mark 6.4; Luke 4.24) for Patrick reads the phrase in its Synoptic context of rejection from homeland and family, and with it the duty to live as a stranger. This passage in the *Epistola*, when read against the related passages in the *Confessio*, shows Patrick as viewing his sense of alienation from home as part of the conformation of his own mind to the mind of Christ; being a stranger is part of the ministry imposed upon him.

We do not know how Patrick imagined the physical world, but we sense that he thought of Ireland and Britain as far apart. Certainly, the actual place of his captivity as a youth is very far from his home: it is a long journey from the Western Sea to where one can sail home (*Confessio* 17), and then there is the barrier of the sea (*Confessio* 18). But if he thinks of those islands as far apart, Britain and Gaul seem very close (*Confessio* 43). A journey to Britain is a major step and one he is unwilling to take once he has returned to Ireland, despite its personal benefits. But if he did go to Britain, then a stay in Gaul with those he desires to see would be one of the added benefits which could be had without difficulty. Distances for an individual's travel are as much a matter of imagination as geography; being in Ireland is dwelling far out from the centre. Going to where the people who matter to him personally live, and then returning, involves what we could call 'excessive travel costs'. It seems that from Ireland to anywhere in the Roman world is a major journey over obstacles and frontiers; but any journey within the empire is just popping in to see the neighbours. Britain and Gaul are imaged as very close together; Britain and Ireland are very far apart.

AN OLD MAN

In view of the quantity of ink used on the question of Patrick's dates of arrival, death, and age at death in this century, any comment on the topic is a fraught matter. The question is: How did Patrick view the Irish episodes within the events of his life? That the two periods in Ireland – first as a slave to a man, then as a slave to the gospel – form the pillars structuring his life's story as presented in the *Confessio* there is no doubt. However, how they relate to one another within his personal sense of time is another matter.

The first period begins when Patrick was about sixteen, and is presented as having all the folly of youth in attendance (*Confessio* 1, 2, 9, 10, 12). Patrick gives us a little information about the length of this first Irish episode: 'Shortly after that I took to flight, left the man with whom I had been for six years, and journeyed . . .' (*Confessio* 17). He presents it as a period of learning, of purification, and of growing to know 'the true God' (*Confessio* 1, 28 and 44 provide examples), so that when he travelled home he was one who prayed and was aware of the workings of the Spirit within him. The early years were a probation and initiation; that he could then leave Ireland is equivalent to a graduation.

Matters become more complicated when it comes to his second trip to Ireland. The sequence of events as noted in the *Confessio* presents his call to go back to Ireland as taking place very soon after his return from slavery (*Confessio* 23), and we imagine that this trip to Ireland was not too long after that again. However, in an earlier place he noted it was 'after many years had gone by' that his mission began (*Confessio* 15). One point seems clear: his life has two significant periods, one in youth, the other in mature age, both in Ireland. The rest of his life, though possibly longer in quantity of time, is less real, no more than duration separating the times in Ireland. His real life is in these two periods which stand out in his mind. It appears that he saw himself as a part of the structure of a greater history; serving a human master in the time of probation, and a divine master (*Confessio* 49) during his mission.

However much this omission of details about his time outside Ireland might frustrate the historian, it does reveal part of the humanity of Patrick. For when we recall our own past we notice that some periods and events stand out from the rest as times of significance. The rest of the time can appear as if the person is standing still with time passing behind in the background. This selection of the important periods of one's life is personal time at its most real.

AT THE ENDS OF THE EARTH

One of the phrases that recurs in Patrick's writing is that he is at 'the very ends of the earth' (*Confessio* 1, 34, 38; *Epistola* 9) or similar expressions. These phrases, which for Patrick locate the position of Ireland, are taken from the New Testament. In Luke 11.31 (parallel Matthew 12.42) Christ tells of the 'queen of the South' who came 'from the ends of the earth' to hear Solomon's wisdom. In Acts 1.8 and 13.47, both of which are in Patrick's mind at the opening of the *Confessio*, 'the ends of the earth' are linked to the preaching of the gospel: the Spirit will make the apostles witnesses to Christ in Jerusalem, the surrounding areas, and 'right out to the end of the earth' (Acts 1.8) and thus the apostles are set up as light for the salvation of the nations 'out to the very end of earth' (Acts 13.47). Moreover, the notion that the gospel is heard 'at the ends of the earth' is also found, but with a different focus, in Romans 10.18 which quotes Psalm 19.4: 'their voice [the heavens' proclamation] goes out through all the earth, and their words to the ends of the world'. So Scripture provides a framework to locate where Patrick finds himself by the will of God. He has been sent to the last place among all the lands, to the furthest-out nation, first by a divine judgement and latterly by a divine commission.

In Luke/Acts we have the story of the early preaching which

presents the message of Jesus spreading through Jerusalem (preaching to Jews); next, through the apostles, to the surrounding areas (also Jews); and then, through the journeys of Paul, reaching 'the nations' (Gentiles) within the Roman Empire. Luke makes clear that this is a three-stage process. This can be represented as a message spreading through three concentric circles. But as Patrick sees it, the limit of the preaching up to his time was the boundary of the empire in the west, but there were a few places even beyond that. Now he has gone out there to the very end, to the nations that are beyond the reach of everyone until then. He is with the nation that is the furthest west (*Confessio* 39) to carry out this commission to teach the nations (*Confessio* 40; *Epistola* 1). Indeed, he has gone beyond where people live (*Confessio* 51), right out to the shore of the Western Sea (*Confessio* 23).

The probability is that Patrick thought the world to be something like this. Towards the centre of the great land mass of the earth was the city of Jerusalem, and around it the promised land. Around this were ranged the nations (cf. Ezekiel 5.5), and their lands stretched out to the ocean. Most of this land mass was held by the Romans but out on the fringe was, at least, one place outside both the orbit of Rome and, as yet, of Jerusalem: Ireland. This was destined to be the outer limit of preaching. That Patrick was thinking in this structural way about his location is confirmed, possibly, by his addition of the other two 'corners' of the earth, north and south, to his citation of Matthew 8:11: 'I tell you, many will come from east and west, and south and north, and sit at table with Abraham, Isaac, and Jacob in the kingdom of heaven' (*Confessio* 39). And the particular people being called, through him, to the banquet is from the extremity of earth (*Confessio* 38). He presents this as the fulfilment of a prophecy in Jeremiah 16.19; and then returns to the Lukan theme of the gospel spreading from Jerusalem by quoting Acts 13.47. Patrick is someone operating out on the final frontier. From one extreme of the world to the other, people are being summoned to the Lord's banquet; Patrick is one of the last offering invitations to the feast of the Lamb. Through his work the message of the gospel, which originated at the centre and had been carried to the nearby nations by the first apostles as recorded in Acts, was brought out in the very last piece of land.

ON THE EDGE OF THE ESCHATON

If Patrick imagines his location as being on the edge, the borders, the last place, of the lands; he has a similar view of his place in history: he belongs to the last times, and the end is imminent. Indeed, the end will not be delayed very long after the completion of his own work in Ireland. He develops this theme in the central section of the *Confessio* by seeing a direct relationship between the preaching of the gospel and the close of human history.

The theme is announced by Patrick thanking God for the task he has been given in 'the last days'. The basis for his belief that these were the final times was that God has promised that he would 'announce his gospel before all nations before the world's end'. Now, Patrick is the instrument of this proclamation, and with his fellow Irish Christians he bears witness to it to the place beyond which no one lives (*Confessio* 34). So we presume that since everywhere has now heard the gospel, there is nothing to delay the end, so it is now close at hand! This reasoning becomes clearer when he restates his position a little further on.

Having announced repeatedly that he has preached the gospel at the ends of the earth, and how thus a prophecy is fulfilled (*Confessio* 37–39), Patrick turns to the basis of all his work: Christ's command to preach (*Confessio* 40). He strings together three roughly parallel texts: first, Matthew 28.19–20 (Go therefore and make disciples of all nations, baptizing them in the name of the Father and of the Son and of the Holy Spirit, teaching them to observe all that I have commanded you; and behold, I am with you all days until the consummation), second, Mark 16.15–16 (Go, therefore, into all the world and preach the gospel to every creature; whoever believes and is baptized will be saved; but whoever does not believe will be condemned), and finally Matthew 24.14 (This gospel of the kingdom will be preached throughout the whole world, as a testimony to all nations; and then will come the end).

As Patrick reads these verses they convey a single structure: preaching followed by completion, preaching followed by judgement, preaching followed by the end. As he reads these verses, the second event – the final judgement that marks the end of the age – is the direct consequence of the completion of the task of preaching. Put simply, once everyone has heard the gospel then there will be no further reason to delay the end. Patrick sees this as the plan in the divine mind for the period between the ascension and the return of Christ in the last times (see *Confessio* 35). Moreover, this vast plan for the history of the world is something that addresses and involves him in a particular way. He is the one who is preaching to the very last nation to hear the message. As such, Patrick sees himself as the final preacher in a chain going back to the apostles. He has had a unique task given to him, for when he has finished his work in Ireland, then the preaching phase of history is finished.

With history complete, the universe enters the next stage in God's plan: the end. And in the very next sentence (*Confessio* 41), Patrick announces the state of history: the gospel has reached Ireland, the outermost place, and those who had only known idols are now 'the prepared people' (Luke 1.17) of the Lord and the children of God. Although Patrick never quotes the verse he seems to have Matthew 10.23 or something like it in mind when formulating his theory ('When they persecute you in one town, flee to the next; for truly, I say to you, you will not have gone through all the towns of Israel, before the Son of man comes'). There is a fixed amount of time before the end; this is determined by the need to preach everywhere, and it is not as great as the length of time needed to get around all the towns of Israel. In any case, there is no need for more time as the given task is completed.

When we reflect on Patrick's humility (*Confessio* 1 and 55, for example) we should remember that he presents himself as having a singular place in bringing about the consummation of creation. With this knowledge we are in a better position for understanding the urgency he must have felt when he referred to living in 'the last days' (*Confessio* 34; and *Epistola* 10). This may also throw light on his expansion of the credal statement, 'who is to come again', to the more pointed, 'and we look forward to his coming in the very near future' (*Confessio* 4).

Patrick saw himself as a stranger in Ireland working on the fringes of human space and time. His work of evangelization belongs to the final, and most difficult, phase of a process that began with the sending out of the apostles by Christ to the whole world (Matthew), starting with Jerusalem and reaching out to every nation out to the very ends of the earth (Luke/Acts). He, Patrick, has carried out successfully his part in this work, so his finishing his work coincides with the completion of the whole apostolic task. The completion of this task ushers in the completion, the judgement, the coming of the Son of Man in glory. So the return of the Christ at the end, foretold in the Scriptures and confessed in the creed, cannot be far in the future in real time.

Four

INTRODUCTION TO THE
CONFESSIO

Patrick has become almost synonymous with Irish Christianity, and indeed with Ireland. Because of this fame more attention has been devoted to him – by religious writers, historians of early Irish history, by philologists and people in many other disciplines – than to any other individual in Irish history. So much indeed, that a forthcoming bibliography will contain several thousand items (Harvey, forthcoming). The effect of this has been that many become more conversant with 'the Patrick problem' than with our most certain evidence: Patrick's own writings. Therefore, the historical problems are left out of consideration here: for them see Chapter 2. By introduction here we need say only this: Patrick was a fifth-century Christian of the Roman Empire, who crossed the sea to an alien land to bring its people Christianity. There, probably late in life, he wrote an account of his life and ministry (see *Confessio* 62).

THE MEANING OF *CONFESSIO*

The title of this work, the *Confessio*, calls for some comment. While the work does not have this title in some early manuscripts, we can consider it an authentic description of what Patrick wanted to write, as he uses the term at the end of the work:

'And this is my declaration (*confessio mea*) before I die.' The meaning of the title, in Latin, is also problematic. Our first instinct is to think of it as a 'confession' in the sense of a reply to his critics – an autobiographical work which fulfils a function somewhat like John Henry Newman's *Apologia pro vita sua* – and such a reply to critics does appear to be part of Patrick's motivation. Another way of looking at the work has been to interpret *confessio* in the sense of a declaration or confession of faith (*confessio/professio fidei*). Again, the expression of his Trinitarian faith lends support to this way of understanding of *confessio*. However, neither of these understandings of *confessio* addresses the fact that many events are retold by Patrick simply because they are seen by him as significant in that they testify to the work of God in his life and deeds.

When we look at various uses of the term *confessio* in the Scriptures in Latin, a different view emerges. It is a praise of the Lord for his strength (Psalm 96.6) and of his majesty and righteousness (Psalm 111.3). It involves telling of the glory which he shares with his people (Psalm 148.14). A confession is a song of God's works, his mighty deeds, and of his mercies towards his people (Psalm 88.2). It is part of the duty of the disciple to offer thanks and acknowledge publicly the gifts of God, that one is in his debt, and that one belongs to him and seeks to do his will in one's actions (Ezra 10.11).

This sense is made even more clear in some passages in the New Testament. Confession is part of holding fast to the work of Christ as the high priest who has made all nations acceptable to the Father (Hebrews 4.14); and this activity of confession is testimony to Christian hope (Hebrews 10.23). It is an aspect of fighting the good fight of the Christian to testify to Christ's saving work in the presence of others (1 Timothy 6.12), and in this the Christian imitates Christ who testified to God's power in the presence of Pilate (1 Timothy 6.13; see John 18.37). If we look on Patrick's account of what God did through him in this light, then his *confessio* is but another part of his own service of God which is the preaching of the gospel to those who have not heard it (see Romans 15.16 and 1 Corinthians 9.12–13).

THE TRANSLATION

The translation is based on the edition of Newport J. D. White (1905), but it takes account of both the edition of Ludwig Bieler (1952) and the work of David Howlett (1994). It has also been compared with many other translations and studies to see where their notes might add to an understanding of the text.

SCRIPTURE CITATIONS AND CANON

It has long been recognized that Patrick used written materials, besides the Scriptures, in this work. For example, Bieler wrote: 'It would certainly be a gross exaggeration to say that he knew no other book than the Bible. There is evidence of his acquaintance with the writings of Sts. Cyprian and Augustine' (*The Works of Saint Patrick*, 1953, p. 15). And more recently, this realization has led to a massive study of possible sources, or at least parallels, of the ideas found in Patrick (Conneely, 1993). While every edition and translation of Patrick has provided a number of biblical references, that of Conneely far outstripped them.

Conneely has been used extensively, but selectively, here; and other references have been added. Hence, the concentration here has been of adding as full a set of biblical references as possible. This strategy's purpose is twofold: first, it shows the extent of Patrick's familiarity with the Scriptures; and second, using the biblical indices given in other works, the reader may compare Patrick's approach with other writers in the Christian tradition regarding the themes upon which he touches.

In every case, the biblical references given are those of the Septuagint/Vulgate. While this is sometimes a little inconvenient, especially with regard to the Psalms, the alternative would have burdened the text with additional notes as many of Patrick's biblical allusions can only be understood in relation to the *Vetus Latina* or Vulgate versions. All translations are made directly from Patrick's Latin rather than adopting an existing translation of the Scriptures. Moreover, it should be noted that the text Patrick used was often different from and longer than that found in many modern editions, including the Vulgate. Where such differences occur, the numeration of the Septuagint is followed. Likewise, it should be noticed that Patrick used the full Greek canon rather than the reduced canon found in many English-language Bibles. All references are, however, treated simply as 'Scripture' as it would be an anachronism to impose upon him the post-sixteenth-century designation of some parts of the traditional Christian Scriptures as 'apocryphal'.

Five

PATRICK'S ACKNOWLEDGEMENT OF GOD'S DEALINGS WITH HIM (The *Confessio*)

Patrick introduces himself and sets his later life in Ireland in the context of his first contact with that island as a captive.

[1] I am the sinner Patrick.[1] I am the most unsophisticated of people, the least of Christians,[2] and for many people I am the most contemptible. My family own a small estate near the village of Bannavem Taburniae. My father was Calpornius, a deacon, and my grandfather was Potitus, a priest. It was near there I was taken captive when I was about sixteen. I was taken into captivity in Ireland – at that time I was ignorant of the true God[3] – along with many thousand others. This was our punishment for departing from God,[4] abandoning his commandments,[5] and ignoring our priests[6] who kept on warning us about our salvation.[7] And 'so' the Lord 'poured upon' us 'the heat of his

[1] Cf. 1 Timothy 1.15.
[2] Cf. Ephesians 3.8.
[3] Cf. John 17.5. If this verse is being echoed in Patrick's writing, which seems most likely, then its meaning is that he had not yet embarked on a way of life that possesses eternal life as its goal.
[4] Cf. Deuteronomy 32.15.
[5] Cf. Genesis 26.5.
[6] Cf. Daniel 9.4–6.
[7] The Latin echoes the Nicene Creed.

anger'[8] and dispersed us among many peoples[9] right 'out to the very ends of the earth'.[10]

God's purpose in punishing is to call the wanderer to conversion; as one who has heard that call, Patrick must pick up the refrain by praising God's loving mercy in his life and sing a confession of faith in God and his actions. His song of praise is his act of thanksgiving for the mercies of God. 'I will sing forever of your mercies, O Lord, from generation to generation my mouth will announce your truth' (Psalm 86.2).

And now it is among the people of that alien land that my smallness[11] is seen. [2] But it was here also the Lord 'opened my understanding to my unbelief',[12] so that even at that late stage I might become aware of my failings.[13] And then remembering my need, I could 'turn with all my heart to the Lord my God'.[14] For it was he who 'looked on my lowliness'[15] and had mercy on the ignorance of my youth,[16] who cared for me[17] before I knew him and before I had gained wisdom or could choose good from evil.[18] It was as a father comforts his son[19] that he protected

[8] Isaiah 42.25.

[9] The notion of dispersal among the nations as a divine punishment for infidelity is found in many places in the Old Testament, e.g. Leviticus 26.33; Ezekiel 4.13; Tobit 13.4–7.

[10] Acts 1.8.

[11] Cf. Jeremiah 45.15; Obadiah 2.

[12] Luke 24.45; Hebrews 3.12.

[13] Cf. Psalm 24.16–18.

[14] Joel 2.12–13.

[15] Luke 1.48.

[16] Cf. Psalm 24.5.

[17] Cf. Psalm 24.7.

[18] 1 Kings 3.9; Genesis 3.5.

[19] Cf. Luke 11.11–13.

me.[20] [**3**] So it would be neither right nor proper[21] to do anything but to tell you all of the many great blessings and grace which the Lord chooses to give me in this land of my captivity.[22] I tell you these things because this is how we return thanks to God,[23] that after being corrected and having come to an awareness of God,[24] that we glorify and bear witness to his wonderful works[25] in the presence of every nation under heaven.[26]

Patrick begins his act of praise/thanksgiving with a formal confession of faith. There has been much discussion as to whether this is the 'creed of Nicea and Constantinople' or not, but all that discussion misses the essential point: creeds were in use in the baptism liturgy and as part of the catechetical process for the first decades of Christianity. By the time of the councils (325 and 381), their basic Trinitarian shape was already fixed in the liturgy and everyday use – it was this practice that gave the councils their model, not the councils which gave a model for ordinary use. Patrick takes over a text of a creed that he knows by heart, that he had used in baptizing and teaching, and since it was his own deepest profession of what he believed, makes it here the basis of his entire recital of God's gifts.

[**4**] For there is not, nor ever was, any other God – there was none before him and there shall not be any after him[27] – besides

---

[20] Cf. Wisdom 4.17.
[21] Cf. 2 Corinthians 12.1.
[22] Cf. 2 Chronicles 6.36–8; Jeremiah 30.16; 46.27.
[23] Cf. Psalm 115.12; 1 Thessalonians 3.9.
[24] Cf. Ephesians 4.14.
[25] Cf. Psalm 88.6.
[26] Cf. Acts 2.5.
[27] Cf. Isaiah 43.10–11.

him who is God the Father unbegotten; without a source, from him everything else takes its beginning. He is, as we say, the one who keeps hold of all things.[28]

And his Son, Jesus Christ, whom we declare to have always existed with the Father, he was with the Father spiritually before the world came into being;[29] begotten of the Father before the beginning of anything in a way that is beyond our speech. And 'through him all things were made',[30] all things visible and invisible.[31] He was made man, and having conquered death was taken back into the heavens to the Father.[32] 'And he has bestowed on him all power above every name in heaven and on earth and under the earth, so that every tongue may confess that our Lord and God is Jesus Christ.'[33] In him we believe, looking forward to his coming in the very near future when he will judge the living and the dead, and 'will repay each according to his works'.[34]

And '[the Father] has plentifully poured upon us the Holy Spirit',[35] the gift and pledge of immortality, who makes those who believe and listen into 'sons of God' the Father 'and fellow heirs with Christ'.[36]

[This is] who we profess and worship, One God in Trinity of sacred name.

[28] Cf. Colossians 1.17.
[29] Cf. John 17.5.
[30] John 1.3.
[31] Cf. Colossians 1.16.
[32] Cf. Mark 16.19.
[33] Philippians 2.9–11.
[34] Romans 2.6.
[35] Titus 3.5–6.
[36] The notion of 'sons' is found in many places in the New Testament (e.g. Matthew 5.9), as is that of 'heirs' (e.g. Galatians 3.29), but the passage behind this phrase of Patrick appears to be Romans 8.14–19.

Patrick turns now to his declaration before his fellow-Christians: a jus-
tification of his life written under the eye of God the judge. In doing
this he is torn: making his testimony known brings the ridicule of men;
not doing it may bring the wrath of God.

[5] As he himself said through the prophet: 'Call upon me in the
day of trouble; I will deliver you, and you shall glorify me.'[37] And
somewhere else: 'It is honourable to acknowledge and reveal the
works of God.'[38] [6] Therefore, though imperfect in many
things, I want my brothers and relatives[39] to know what kind of
person I am. Then they can understand the way I have spent my
life. [7] I am not forgetting 'the testimony of' my 'Lord'[40] who
declares in the Psalms: 'You destroy those who speak lies'[41] and
who elsewhere says: 'The lying mouth kills the soul.'[42] Nor that
the same Lord says in the gospel: 'I tell you, on the day of judgement people will render account for every careless word they
utter.'[43] [8] So with all my heart I dread, 'with fear and trem-
bling',[44] that sentence on the Day of Judgement.[45] And, no one
can avoid[46] that day when each of us shall 'render an account' of
even the least sins 'before the judgement seat of' the Lord
'Christ'.[47] [9] This is why I have thought of writing my story for

[37] Psalm 49.15.
[38] Tobit 12.7.
[39] Cf. Luke 21.16.
[40] 2 Timothy 1.8.
[41] Psalm 5.7.
[42] Wisdom 1.11.
[43] Matthew 12.36.
[44] Ephesians 6.5.
[45] Cf. Isaiah 24.21; Jeremiah 25.33; Romans 2.16; Luke 10.12.
[46] Cf. Genesis 3.10; 4.9.
[47] Romans 14.10, 12.

a long while, but held back until now out of fear of men's tongues, and because – unlike others – I have not been one of those students who in the very best manner has drunk both law and sacred letters.[48] They have never had to change their speech since infancy; rather they were always improving and perfecting their command of language. My words and speech,[49] however, are turned into an alien language, and you can see my literary quality with a glance at my writing. As the wise man says: 'For wisdom becomes known through speech, and education through the words of the tongue.'[50]

[10] But what use is even a true excuse, especially when there is an element of presumption in it? Now, as an old man, I desire what I missed in youth when my sins stopped me from grasping what I was reading. But even if I shout this out, will anyone believe me? When I was taken captive, I was young – almost a speechless boy – and did not yet know what I ought to desire and what to avoid. Now today it is with great fear and shame that I expose my lack of expertise and polish. So here is my position: to the learned I am unable to make my meaning clear[51] with the brevity my spirit and mind desire and the disposition towards which my understanding points.[52] [11] But if I had been given the same chance as the rest, then without a doubt,

[48] Cf. 2 Timothy 3.14–15.
[49] Cf. John 8.43.
[50] Sirach 4.29.
[51] Cf. Ecclesiastes 1.8.
[52] This sentence, and especially the last part of it, is unclear. It baffled medieval readers, whose suggestions have further baffled modern editors! What is given here is a rendering that seeks to reflect the overall direction of the sentence.

'for the sake of the reward',[53] 'I' would 'not keep silent'.[54] And, if it seems to some that I am being arrogant in making my declaration – I lacking learning and spoke with a 'slow tongue'[55] – then note that it is written: 'The tongue of the stammerers will learn quickly to speak peace.'[56] This should be our main desire; we who are, as it says, 'the letter of Christ for salvation unto the uttermost parts of the earth'.[57] And, although this letter is not learned, it is 'one delivered' with strength, 'written in our hearts not with ink, but with the Spirit of the living God'.[58] And again, 'the Spirit bears witness':[59] 'For the Most High also created the things of the farmyard.'[60]

Patrick begins his history by reflecting on what he is doing: telling this story is part of his ministry and it is a gift to other believers. But we will discover this is a complex fabric. It interweaves his story of his actions, others' actions, and God's action. It is the history of salvation for him personally which is an interweaving of God's invitations and his responses. And this small-scale, personal history of salvation is interwoven with the large-scale history of salvation: the divine plan for the creation.

[12] So at first, I was a rustic and a wanderer[61] without any

[53] Psalm 118.112.

[54] Isaiah 62.1.

[55] Exodus 4.10.

[56] Isaiah 32.4. This reading is found only in the Septuagint and *Vetus Latina.*

[57] A conflation of 2 Corinthians 3.2–3 and Acts 13.47.

[58] 2 Corinthians 3.2–3.

[59] Hebrews 10.15; and see John 15.25; Romans 8.16; 1 John 5.7.

[60] Sirach 7.16.

[61] This word, *profuga,* is an echo.of Cain sent off to wander (Genesis 4.12); it seems that Patrick is seeing himself as like Cain, sent into a foreign land away from his family as a punishment for his sins; cf. *Address to the Soldiers of Coroticus,* n. 1.

learning 'who knew not how to provide for what would come later'.[62] But I know one thing with certainty: that 'before I was punished'[63] I was like a stone lying in the deepest mire;[64] and then, 'he who is mighty'[65] came and, in his mercy, raised me up.[66] He most truly raised me on high and set me on the top of the rampart.[67] So I shout out and thank the Lord. His blessings are truly great, here and in eternity, and beyond all we can imagine. [13] Now, be amazed 'you both small and great who fear God'.[68] All you learned ones, you sophisticated speakers, listen and study what you hear! Who was it that raised up a fool like me from among you who seem so wise, from you who 'experts in the law'[69] and are 'powerful in word'[70] and everything else? It was God who breathed his life into me (the detestable of this world[71] – if that is what I am) above others in order that I should faithfully serve, 'with fear and reverence'[72] and 'without blame',[73] the people to whom Christ's love brought me.[74] Indeed, God gave me – should I be found worthy of the commission – to this people for the rest of my days. In short his wish is that I should serve them truly with humility.[75] [14] So it is right and

[62] Ecclesiastes 4.13.
[63] Psalm 118.67.
[64] Cf. Psalm 68.2, 15.
[65] Luke 1.49.
[66] Cf. Psalm 114.14.
[67] Cf. Psalm 112.7–8.
[68] Revelation 19.5.
[69] Luke 7.30.
[70] Luke 24.19.
[71] Cf. 1 Corinthians 1.20; 3.19.
[72] Hebrews 12.28.
[73] That holy people live without blame is a theme found in the wisdom literature – (e.g. Wisdom 10.5; Sirach 8.10) – and in Paul – (e.g. Philippians 2.15; 3.6).
[74] Cf. 2 Corinthians 5.14.
[75] Cf. Acts 20.19.

proper 'in the measure of faith'[76] in the Trinity, to make known clearly 'the gift of God'[77] and his 'eternal consolation'.[78] And, do this 'without hesitating'[79] at its dangers. Equally it is proper to spread abroad 'the name of God',[80] with trust and 'without fear',[81] so that even 'after my death'[82] I may leave something of value to the many thousands, my brothers and sisters, sons and daughters, I have baptized in the Lord. **[15]** I was not worthy[83] in any way for what the Lord was to grant this servant after tribulations and setbacks, captivity, and many long years. God chose to give me a great grace towards that people [who had held me captive], but this was something I had never thought of, nor hoped for, in my youth.

In describing life when a slave to Ireland, Patrick recounts his first encounter with God. God's prompting leads him to pray, and in this new relationship Patrick sees the Spirit inspiring and directing him. It is a time of spiritual growth given him by God, and it has in his eyes the purity and simplicity of a spiritual 'honeymoon'. His relationship with God lacks the complexity, difficulties, and darknesses that beset him in his mature life as a Christian and a minister.

[16] But then, when I had arrived in Ireland and was looking after flocks the whole time, I prayed frequently each day. And

---

[76] Romans 12.3.
[77] John 4.10.
[78] Cf. 2 Thessalonians 2.16.
[79] Cf. Philippians 2.15.
[80] 2 Esdras 2.45 = IV Esdras 2.45 in the appendix to the Vulgate.
[81] Philippians 1.14.
[82] 2 Peter 1.15.
[83] Cf. Matthew 8.8.

more and more,[84] the love of God and the fear of him grew in me, and my faith was increased[85] and my spirit enlivened.[86] So much so that I prayed up to a hundred times in the day, and almost as often at night. I even remained in the wood and on the mountain to pray. And – come hail, rain or snow – I was up before dawn to pray, and I sensed no evil nor spiritual laziness within.[87] I now understand this: at that time 'the Spirit was fervent'[88] in me.

[17] And it was there, indeed, that one night I heard a voice which said to me: 'Well have you fasted. Very soon you are to travel to your homeland.' And again, not long after that, I heard 'a revelation'[89] which said to me: 'Behold! Your ship is prepared.' But the ship was far, perhaps two hundred miles away. I had never been, nor knew anybody, there. Shortly after that I fled the man I had been with for six years. At last I arrived at the ship. I had travelled[90] 'in the power of God',[91] he directed my path[92] towards the good, and I feared nothing.[93]

Now for the first time we hear Patrick describing how he interacted with others. He acknowledges the name of Christian. As he looks back from

[84] Cf. Philippians 1.9.
[85] Cf. Luke 17.5.
[86] Cf. Romans 8.14.
[87] Cf. Daniel 3.52–90, see Higgins, 1995.
[88] Acts 18.25.
[89] Romans 11.4. This word responsus in Paul – NRSV uses 'a divine reply' – is used by Patrick for what is said by God during or after a vision. When it occurs, I translate it by 'a revelation'.
[90] The Latin echoes 1 Corinthians 2.1.
[91] 1 Corinthians 2.5.
[92] Cf. Tobit 4.20; 1 Thessalonians 3.11.
[93] Cf. Psalm 22.4.

the time of writing he sees the interweaving of his life and the divine plan grow more intense. His actions are presented as part of this plan, and God stands with him in his difficulties, for in them God reveals himself to those who are without knowledge of salvation. Patrick presents his own life as the instrument by which God makes himself present to other people who have not yet heard God's name.

[**18**] On the day I arrived, the ship was about to go and I told them I wanted to sail with them from there. But this displeased the captain who, with disdain, replied: 'No way can you ask to travel with us!' So I went away from them to a hut where I could shelter. On the way I began to pray, and before I finished my prayer I heard a crewman shouting loudly to me: 'Come! Quickly! These men are calling you.' I turned back at once and they said: 'Come on, we are taking you on trust. So show your friendship with us according to whatever custom you choose.' But on that day I refused to suck their nipples,[94] on account of the fear of God,[95] yet despite this I stayed with them for I hoped that some of them would come to faith in Jesus Christ – for they all belonged to 'the nations'.[96] At once we got under way. [**19**] We landed after three days, and then for twenty-eight days we made our way through a desert. Their food ran out, and

---

[94] This phrase has troubled editors and translators of Patrick for centuries. In fact, 'to suck the nipples' is an Old Irish expression, and no doubt a symbolic practice as well, describing the appeal of an inferior for the protection and friendship of a superior. The significance of Patrick's refusal was that he did not want to enter into a formal agreement of protection with them – i.e. he denied them his intimate friendship – as they were pagans.

[95] Nehemiah 5.15.

[96] For what we call 'pagans', Patrick uses the biblical word – see Matthew 28.19 for an example.

starvation came over them.[97] Just then the captain asked me: 'So now Christian, you explain to us why we are in this mess. Your God is great and all powerful,[98] so why can't you pray for us? We are on the very brink with hunger and it seems unlikely we will ever see another human being.' So I boldly said to them: '"Turn" in trust and "with your whole heart"[99] to the Lord, my God, to whom nothing is impossible,[100] that today he may send food to satisfy you on your journey – for he has an abundance everywhere.'[101] Then, with God's help, it happened. Behold, a herd of swine appeared before our eyes on the road,[102] and they killed many of them. They made camp there for two nights and, with their fill of pork, they were well restored for many of them had dropped out[103] and had been left half dead by the roadside.[104] After this they thanked God mightily, I became honourable in their eyes,[105] and they had an abundance of food. They also came across some wild honey[106] and 'offered some of it'[107] to me. Then one of them said: 'This has been offered as a sacrifice.'[108] But thanks be to God, I had tasted none of it.

It is significant for Patrick's understanding of the trials of the Christian

[97] Cf. Genesis 12.10.
[98] Cf. Deuteronomy 10.17.
[99] Joel 2.12.
[100] Luke 1.37.
[101] Cf. Exodus 16.12.
[102] Cf. Matthew 8.28–30.
[103] Cf. Matthew 15.32.
[104] Cf. Luke 10.30.
[105] This motif is found in several places in Scripture: the prophet shows the power of God to the Gentiles, and so is honoured by them – e.g. 2 Kings 5.
[106] Cf. Matthew 3.4.
[107] Luke 24.42.
[108] Cf. 1 Corinthians 10.28.

life that he sees a connection between this first occasion when he is responsible for people praising God and his first trial by the devil. This connection between testing and temptation is made frequently by reference to the advice of the son of Sirach: 'My son, if you wish to be the Lord's servant, prepare yourself for testing' (2.1).

[20] It was that night, while I was asleep, that Satan strongly tried me – I shall remember it 'as long as I am in the body'.[109] Something like an enormous rock fell on top of me and I lost all power over my limbs. At that time I was ignorant about the spiritual side of life, so how did I know I should call on Helias?[110] At that very instant I saw the sun rise in the sky, while I called out 'Helia, Helia' with all my strength. Then the sun's splendour fell on me and instantly dispelled all the crushing weight. I believe that Christ, my Lord, assisted me; and that it was his Spirit who cried out through me.[111] And I hope it will be so again 'in the day of my distress'[112] as the Gospel says: 'On that day' the Lord declares, 'it is not you who speak, but the Spirit of your Father who will speak in you'.[113]

This part of the Confessio *is reminiscent of the Exodus experience of the chosen people travelling through the desert wilderness: it is a time of*

[109] 2 Peter 1.13.

[110] This is one of the knottiest problems in Patrick. Is he calling on the sun as a god or as a divine sacrament – the Greek for sun is Helios? Or is he calling on Elijah – (H)elias in Latin? Some who heard Christ calling out on the cross thought he was calling on Elijah – cf. Matthew 27.46–7.

[111] Cf. Romans 8.26.

[112] Psalm 49.15.

[113] Matthew 10.19–20.

spiritual testing while on a difficult physical trip, during which the Lord provides for the wanderers and Patrick acts as their Moses-like intercessor.

[22][114] And as we travelled [the Lord] looked after us with food, fire and dry shelter each day, until after fourteen days[115] we came into human society. As I said already, we marched for twenty-eight days through the desert and on the night we reached humanity, all that food was gone.[116]

This next, curious passage seems to imply that Patrick was taken captive a second time, but that is all we know. However, to whatever historical event it refers, it once again shows Patrick viewing his life as one in which God is continually revealing his salvation.

[21] And after many years, I was once again taken captive. But on the very first night I was with them, I heard a divine revelation[117] which said to me: 'You will remain with them for two months.' This is just what happened: on the sixtieth night, 'the Lord freed me from their hands'.[118]

Patrick recounts his call to go back to the Irish and preach the gospel. The account has several calls coming to him at night – it is reminiscent

---

[114] In all the manuscripts, 21 follows at this point, where it clearly does not belong as it interrupts the story of what happened on the twenty-eight days in 'the desert' from leaving the ship to reaching civilization. Some editors leave it in sequence but place it in brackets. However, it is clear that it belongs later than the days in the desert, but before he received his mission to Ireland. Therefore, between 22 and 23 seems a likely place.

[115] Some manuscripts read: 'after ten days'.

[116] Cf. Joshua 5.12.

[117] Romans 11.4.

[118] Genesis 37.21.

*of the call of Samuel (1 Samuel 3) – before he finally recognizes what
he should do. Although Patrick gives us no direct information on when
this happened, when we piece together several hints in the text it is
not unreasonable to assume that this vocation may have been several
decades after his first escape. His mid-forties, or even later, would fit all
the evidence.*

[**23**] And after a few years I was again with my parents in Britain
who welcomed me home as a son. They begged me in good
faith after all my adversities to go nowhere else, nor ever leave
them again.

The first call

And it was there, I speak the truth, that 'I saw a vision of the
night':[119] a man named Victoricus – 'like one'[120] from Ireland –
coming with innumerable letters. He gave me one of them and
I began to read what was in it: 'The voice of the Irish'. And just
as I was reading the letter's opening, I thought I heard the voices
of those who live around the wood of Foclut which is close to
the Western Sea. It was 'as if they were shouting with one
voice':[121] 'O holy boy, we beg you to come again and walk
among us.' And I was 'broken-hearted'[122] and could not read
more. Then I woke up. Thank God, after many years the Lord
granted them what they called out for.

[119] Daniel 7.13.
[120] Daniel 7.13.
[121] Daniel 3.51.
[122] Psalm 108.16; cf. Acts 2.37.

The second call

[**24**] And on another night, either in me or close to me – 'I do not know, God knows'[123] – I heard them using the most learned words. But I could not understand them, except what became clear towards the end of the speech: 'He who "gave his life"[124] for you, he it is who speaks in you.' And at that point I woke, and was full of joy.

The third call, followed by recognition of the Spirit's activity

[**25**] And yet again I saw him praying in me, and it was as if I was inside my body and I heard [him] over me, that is over 'the inner man'[125] and he was praying there powerfully with sighs.[126] And in my excitement and astonishment[127] I wondered who it could be that was praying in me? But towards the end of the prayer it became clear that it was the Spirit. Just then I awoke and remembered what was said through the apostle: 'Likewise the Spirit helps the weaknesses of our prayers; for we do not know how to pray as we ought, but the Spirit himself intercedes for us with sighs beyond what words can express.'[128] And again Scripture says: 'The Lord is our Advocate,[129] he intercedes for us'.[130]

---

[123] 2 Corinthians 12.2.
[124] Cf. John 10.11.
[125] Ephesians 3.16; Romans 7.22.
[126] Cf. Romans 8.26.
[127] Cf. Isaiah 29.9; Acts 2.12; 8.13.
[128] Romans 8.26.
[129] Cf. 1 John 2.1.
[130] Romans 8.27, 34.

The focus now moves from Patrick's call, to go back to Ireland, to the challenge that was made to him when aged about forty-five that he was unworthy of an office in the church. The whole passage is anything but clear: What was the 'sin' he refers to? Why did they consider him unworthy of office? Where and by whom was the challenge brought? Was Patrick physically present at a trial, and indeed what was the outcome of the challenge? All we can say is this: before he was taken captive – at the time when he did not 'know the true God' (a point he emphasizes here and at the beginning of the Confessio; *and cf. John 17.5) – he committed a sinful act. He was then punished by God for this and did his penance by suffering during his first captivity; there he came to his spiritual senses and discovered how he should live and act. Now, years later, it is held against him and his reply is that he was not really aware of his actions at that time, that he had made public acknowledgement of it before he was a deacon, and has undergone the divine cleansing of chastisement by his captivity in Ireland.*

However, it appears that Patrick's arguments did not succeed and he was rejected. Yet at this point Patrick speaks with new assurance, for in all these trials the Lord is with him. Patrick discovers a new level of divine support, for the Lord identifies himself with Patrick and his sufferings.

[26] And when I was tested by some of my superiors who opposed my toilsome office of bishop with my sins – truly on that day 'I was struck' mightily 'so that I was falling'[131] here and in eternity – then did the Lord in his goodness spare the convert

[131] Psalm 117.13.

and the stranger 'for his name's sake'.[132] And he powerfully came to my aid in this battering so that I did not slip badly into the wreckage of sin nor into infamy. I pray God that 'it may not be charged against them'[133] as sin. [27] 'The charge they brought'[134] against me was something from thirty years earlier which I had admitted before I was even made a deacon. Once when I was anxious and worried I hinted to my dearest friend about something I had done one day – indeed in one hour – in my youth, for I had not then prevailed over my sinfulness. 'I do not know, God knows'[135] if I was then fifteen years old, and I was not a believer in the true God[136] nor had I ever been,[137] but I 'remained in death'[138] and 'non-belief'[139] until I was truly punished[140] and, in truth, brought low by daily deprivations of hunger and nakedness.[141]

[28] Against [the charge I could point out that] I continued on in Ireland, not of my own volition, until I almost perished. But this [captivity] was very good for me for I was corrected by the Lord; and he prepared me for what I am today – a state I

---

[132] Psalm 106.8, but while the notion of being delivered from trial for the Lord's name's sake is found in the Synoptics, it is the verbal form of Psalm 106 that Patrick has in mind: cf. Matthew 19.29; 24.9. Patrick sees himself in the tribulation prophesied in the Gospel.

[133] 2 Timothy 4.16. Patrick sees himself as one opposed in a trial, as Paul says he was opposed by Alexander the coppersmith – 2 Timothy 4.14–17.

[134] Daniel 6.5.

[135] 2 Corinthians 12.2.

[136] Cf. John 17.5.

[137] Literally: 'nor [had I believed] since my infancy'.

[138] 1 John 3.14.

[139] Romans 11.23; 1 Timothy 1.13 – Patrick again appeals to Paul as a precedent for his own life.

[140] Cf. Psalm 117.18.

[141] Cf. Deuteronomy 28.48; 2 Corinthians 11.27.

was then far away from – when I have many duties and pastoral care for the salvation of others, but at that time I was not even concerned for myself.

[**29**] And so came the day when I was rejected[142] by those I have mentioned; and on that night: 'I saw a vision of the night'.[143] [I saw] a piece of writing without any nobility opposite my face, and at the same time I heard a divine revelation[144] saying: 'We have seen with anger the face of the chosen one with his name laid bare [of respect].' Note he did not say: 'You have seen with anger', but 'We have seen with anger', as if he were joined on to his chosen one. As he said: 'He who touches you touches the pupil of my eye.'[145] [**30**] So it is that 'I give thanks to him who strengthened me'[146] in all things: that he did not impede me in my chosen journey, nor in my works which I had learned from Christ my Lord. On the contrary, I felt in myself a strength, by no means small, coming from him,[147] and that my 'faith was proven in the presence of God and men'.[148] [**31**] And so 'I boldly declare'[149] that my conscience is clear both now and in the future. I have 'God as [my] witness'[150] that I am not a liar[151] in those things that I have told you.

[**32**] But I am very sorry for my dearest friend, to whom I

---

[142] Cf. Psalm 117.22.

[143] Daniel 7.13.

[144] Romans 11.4.

[145] Zechariah 2.8.

[146] 1 Timothy 1.12.

[147] The language and ideas reflect Mark 5.27–30.

[148] Sirach 25.1; and cf. 1 Peter 1.7; 2 Corinthians 8.21.

[149] Acts 2.29.

[150] Romans 1.9 – a phrase used on several occasions by Paul.

[151] Cf. Galatians 1.20.

trusted even my soul, that we had to hear this revelation.[152] And I found out from some of the brethren that at the enquiry he fought for me in my absence. (I was not present at it, nor was I in Britain, nor did the issue arise from me.) He indeed it was who told me with his own lips: 'Behold, you are to be given the rank of bishop' – something for which I was unworthy. So how did he later come to the idea of disgracing me in public in the presence of all those people both good and bad, [regarding a matter] which earlier he had, joyfully and of his own volition, pardoned me, as indeed had the Lord who is greater than all?[153] [**33**] Enough said!

Patrick's task is to get on with his mission of professing Christ's love, and uniting his life to Christ by offering himself as his minister. Patrick must persevere in this despite the questions, doubts and criticisms of friends, family and other clerics. His own mission in Ireland is part of the universal plan of salvation that the gospel must be preached in every place out to the ends of the earth, so that history may be brought to its completion with the return of Christ.

However, I must not hide that gift of God which he gave us bountifully in the land of my captivity,[154] because it was then that I fiercely sought him and there found him and he preserved me from all iniquities.[155] I believe this to be so because of his

[152] Cf. Romans 11.4.
[153] Cf. John 10.29.
[154] Cf. 2 Chronicles 6.36–8.
[155] Cf. Sirach 33.1; 2 Timothy 1.12, combined with a common scriptural expression, e.g. used at Leviticus 16.21–2.

Spirit dwelling in me[156] who has worked in me[157] until this very day.[158] This is something I will boldly repeat.[159] But God knows that if a man had said this to me, perhaps then I would have remained silent[160] because of Christ's love.[161] **[34]** And so I thank my God without ceasing[162] who preserved me as his faithful one 'on the day of' my 'trial'[163] so that today I can offer a sacrifice to him with confidence. [Today] I offer my soul as 'a living victim'[164] to Christ my Lord who 'preserved me in all my troubles'[165] so that I can say: '"Who am I, O Lord"[166] and what is my vocation, that you have cooperated with me with such divine [power]?'

Thus today I constantly praise and glorify your name[167] wherever I may be among the nations[168] both in my successes and my difficulties. So whatever happens to me – good or ill – I ought to accept with an even temper[169] and 'always give thanks to God'[170] who has shown me that I can trust him without limit or doubt. It is he who 'in the last days'[171] heard me, so that I – an ignorant man – should dare to take up so holy and wonderful a

[156] Cf. Romans 8.11.
[157] Cf. 1 Corinthians 12.11.
[158] This is a common scriptural expression – see, e.g., Joshua 16.10.
[159] Cf. Acts 2.29.
[160] Cf. Proverbs 11.12; Amos 5.13.
[161] Cf. 2 Corinthians 5.14.
[162] Cf. 1 Corinthians 1.4.
[163] Psalm 94.9; cf. Wisdom 3.18.
[164] Romans 12.1.
[165] Psalm 33.5–7.
[166] 2 Samuel 7.18.
[167] Cf. Psalm 33.4; Psalm 45.11; Sirach 33.10.
[168] This notion is found in many places in the Scriptures – e.g. Psalm 17.49; Isaiah 12.4; Ezekiel 20.9; Malachi 1.11; Revelation 15.4; etc. – but Patrick may be thinking especially of 2 Samuel 7.23 as this part of 2 Samuel is used a few lines earlier.
[169] Cf. Job 2.10.
[170] 2 Thessalonians 1.3; 2.13.
[171] Acts 2.17.

work as this: that I should in some way imitate those[172] to whom the Lord foretold what was about to occur when 'his gospel [of the kingdom will be preached throughout the whole world], as a testimony to all nations' before the end of the world.[173] And this is what we see. It has been fulfilled.[174] Behold! We are [now] witnesses to the fact that the gospel has been preached out to beyond where anyone lives.[175]

[35] To narrate in detail[176] either the whole story of my labours or even parts of it would take a long time. So, lest I injure my readers, I shall tell you briefly how God, the all-holy one, often freed me from slavery and from twelve dangers which threatened my life, as well as from many snares and from things which I am unable to express in words.[177] Moreover, I have God as my authority – he who knows all things even before they happen – that he frequently warned me, a poor ignorant orphan, through divine revelations.[178] [36] So where did I get this wisdom?[179] It was not in me: I neither knew the number of [my] days[180] nor cared about God. Where did I later get that great and health-giving gift that I might know and love God, albeit that I had to leave my country and parents? [37] And many gifts were

---

[172] This notion of sanctity/discipleship as imitating models of holiness is a theme in Paul, and a particular theme in Patrick's understanding of holiness, cf. nn. 42, 47 and 59 – where there is a fuller comment on the theme.

[173] Matthew 24.14. He paraphrases the final phrase using a word from Matthew 24.13; there is also an echo of the notion of 'the ends of the earth' from Acts 1.8.

[174] James 2.23; cf. Matthew 24.14.

[175] Cf. Acts 1.8.

[176] Acts 21.19.

[177] Cf. Romans 8.26.

[178] Romans 11.4.

[179] Matthew 13.54.

[180] Cf. Psalm 38.5; Job 38.21.

offered to me with sorrow and tears. And I offended them and went against the will not only of some of my elders but, under God's direction, I refused to consent or agree with them in any way. It was not my grace, but God who conquered in me and who resisted them all that I might come 'to the Irish nations to preach the gospel'[181] and put up with insults from unbelievers, that I might 'hear the hatred of the wanderer',[182] [endure] many persecutions even including chains,[183] and that I should give up my freedom for the benefit of others. And, indeed, if I be worthy I am ready to give my life right now[184] 'for his name's sake'.[185] And, if the Lord should grant it to me,[186] it is there [in Ireland] I want 'to spend freely'[187] my life 'even until death'.[188]

Patrick is thankful that he has succeeded in his given task and will stay at his post until the Lord's coming in glory. He has preached the word in Ireland and it has taken root, and is bearing much fruit.

[38] Truly, I am greatly in God's debt.[189] He has given me a great

---

[181] Cf. Mark 13.10. Patrick says that he came 'to preach the gospel to the Irish nations' – *ad Hibernas gentes euangelium praedicare* – while Mark 13.10 reads that 'the gospel must be preached to all the nations' – *in omnes gentes primum oportet praedicari euangelium*. The change from the passive to the active voice is significant, given Patrick's overall sense of his part in fulfilling what is commanded about preaching in the Gospels. Jesus spoke about what has to have taken place before the eschaton; Patrick is setting out to help in accomplishing this result.

[182] Sirach 29.30. On Patrick's use of this verse in combination with Mark 13.10, see Chapter 3.

[183] 2 Timothy 2.9.

[184] Cf. John 13.37.

[185] Cf. Romans 1.5.

[186] Cf. Isaiah 26.15.

[187] Cf. 2 Corinthians 12.15.

[188] Cf. Philippians 2.8.

[189] Cf. Romans 1.14.

grace, that through me many peoples might be reborn[190] and later brought to completion;[191] and also that from among them everywhere clerics should be ordained [to serve] this people – who have but recently come to belief – [and] which the Lord has taken [to himself] 'from the ends of the earth'.[192] He thus fulfilled 'what he once promised through his prophets':[193] 'to you shall the nations come from the ends of the earth and say "Our fathers have inherited nought but lies, worthless things in which there is no profit."'[194] And in another place:[195] 'I have set you to be a light for the nations, that you may bring salvation to the uttermost parts of the earth'.[196]

[39] And it is there [in Ireland] that I desire 'to wait for the promise'[197] of him who never deceives us and who repeatedly promises in the Gospel: 'They will come from the east and from the west and from the south and from the north and sit at table with Abraham, Isaac, and Jacob.'[198] So we believe that believers will come from the whole world.

[40] So it is right and proper that we should fish well and carefully – as the Lord warns and teaches us, saying: 'Come after

[190] Cf. John 3.5.
[191] Cf. 2 Corinthians 8.6; Hebrews 11.40; Revelation 15.8.
[192] Jeremiah 16.19.
[193] Romans 1.2.
[194] Jeremiah 16.19.
[195] Cf. John 19.37, which is the model for Patrick's use of Scripture here. In John, two verses are quoted in a catena (i.e. a chain of scriptural quotations) and it is this combination which is brought to fulfilment. Here Patrick uses the same device; and even echoes John's language.
[196] Acts 13.47.
[197] Acts 1.4.
[198] Matthew 8.11. It should be noted that Patrick adds the two other corners of the world – south and north – to the gospel text.

me and I shall make you fishers of men.'[199] And again[200] he says through the prophets: 'Behold! I send out fishermen and many hunters, says God',[201] and so forth. So truly it is our task to cast our nets[202] and catch 'a great multitude'[203] and crowd for God; and [to make sure] that there are clergy everywhere to baptize and preach to a people who are in want and in need. This is exactly what the Lord warns and teaches about in the Gospel when he says: 'Go therefore, and teach all the nations, baptizing them in the name of the Father and of the Son and of the Holy Spirit, teaching them to observe all that I have commanded you; and behold, I am with you always, even to the close of the age.'[204] And again:[205] 'Go into all the world and preach the gospel to the entire universe. Whoever believes and is baptized will be saved; but whoever does not believe will be condemned.'[206] And again:[207] 'this gospel of the kingdom will be preached throughout the entire universe, as a testimony to all nations; and then the end will come'.[208]

And likewise the Lord foretold this through the prophet when he says: 'And in the last days it shall be, says the Lord, that I will pour out my Spirit upon all flesh, and your sons and your

[199] Matthew 4.19.
[200] Cf. John 19.37.
[201] Jeremiah 16.16.
[202] Cf. Mark 1.16; John 21.11.
[203] Luke 6.17; cf. Luke 5.6.
[204] Matthew 28.19–20. Note his added emphasis of urgency: 'Go therefore now . . .'
[205] Cf. John 19.37.
[206] Mark 16.15–16. I have rendered *uniuersus mundus* as 'entire universe', as this cosmological nuance is present in the original and in the Latin, but is not captured by a phrase like 'whole world' or 'all creation'.
[207] Cf. John 19.37.
[208] Matthew 24.14.

daughters shall prophesy, and your young men shall see visions, and your old men shall dream dreams; and indeed on my menservants and my maidservants in those days I will pour out my Spirit; and they shall prophesy.'[209] And the prophet Hosea says: 'Those who were not my people I will call "my people", and her who was not beloved I will call "my beloved". And in the very place where it was said to them, "You are not my people", they will be called "sons of the living God"'.[210] **[41]** Such indeed is the case in Ireland where they never had knowledge of God[211] – and until now they celebrated only idols and unclean things.[212]

The proof that Patrick's mission is from God is the fruit it has produced. This is the answer to those who declared him unfit and appear to have wanted him to leave Ireland to come and answer their charges. Patrick, it seems, has ignored their summons and tells them of the difficulties and success of his work instead.

Yet recently, what a change: they have become 'a prepared people'[213] of the Lord, and they are now called 'the sons of God'.[214] And the Irish leaders' sons and daughters are seen to become the monks and virgins of Christ.[215] **[42]** Indeed, on one occasion

---

[209] Acts 2.17–18; cf. Joel 2.28–9.

[210] Romans 9.25–6. Note that it is Paul who says this is Hosea; cf. Hosea 1.9–10; 2.1; 2.23. Cf. also **59**.

[211] Cf. Romans 1.28.

[212] This notion in Patrick reflects Paul's thinking in Romans 1.19–24 – cf. 2 Kings 17.12.

[213] Cf. Luke 1.17.

[214] Cf. 1 John 3.1 – and Romans 8.14; 9.26.

[215] The word 'virgin' means here something similar to 'nun'.

this happened. A blessed Irish woman of noble birth, a most beautiful adult whom I had baptized, came back to us a few days later for this reason. She told us how she had received a divine communication[216] from a messenger of God which advised her to become a virgin of Christ and that she should move closer to God. Thanks be to God, six days after that she avidly and commendably took up[217] that life which is lived by all who are virgins of God. This, of course, is not to the liking of their fathers and they have to suffer persecution and false accusation from their parents.[218] Yet despite this their number keeps increasing and we do not know the number of those born there from our begetting – apart from widows and those who are celibate. But of all these women, those held in slavery have to work hardest; they are continually harassed and even have to suffer being terrorized. But the Lord gives grace to many of his maidservants, and the more they are forbidden to imitate[219] [the Lord], the more they boldly do this.

[**43**] This, therefore, is the situation: even if I were willing to leave them and go to Britain – and I was all set[220] to go there, and wanted to go, for it is my homeland and where my family is – and Gaul 'to visit the brethren'[221] and see the face of my Lord's saints – God knows how much I wanted to do this – I am 'bound in the Spirit', who 'testifies to me'[222] that should I do

[216] Cf. Acts 10.22; Romans 11.4.
[217] Cf. Matthew 11.12.
[218] Cf. Luke 21.16.
[219] This is an echo of the Pauline notion of imitating Christ as being the guide to Christian behaviour; cf. the notes on **59** where there is a fuller comment and references.
[220] Cf. Psalm 118.60.
[221] Acts 7.23; 15.36.
[222] Acts 20.22, 23.

this he would view me as guilty. Moreover, I fear the loss of the work I have begun here, since it is not I but Christ the Lord who has ordered me to come [here] and be with these people for the rest of my life. If the Lord wills it,[223] he will guard my way from every evil,[224] that I might not sin in his presence.[225] [**44**] However, I hope I have done the right thing, for 'as long as I am in this body of death'[226] I do not trust myself because he is strong[227] who daily tries to drag me away from faith and from the genuine religious chastity which I have chosen for Christ my Lord until the end of my life. But the hostile flesh[228] is always drawing me towards death,[229] namely, towards doing those enticing things which are forbidden. While I know in part[230] those matters where I have had a less perfect life than other believers, I do acknowledge this to my Lord and I am not ashamed[231] in his sight[232] – 'for I do not lie'.[233] From the time I knew him, from youth,[234] the love of God and the fear of him have grown within me so that, with the Lord's help, 'I have kept the faith'[235] until now.[236]

[223] Cf. James 4.15.
[224] Cf. Psalm 118.101.
[225] Cf. Luke 15.18, 21.
[226] 2 Peter 1.13; Romans 7.24.
[227] The 'strong one' is Satan. The identification is based on Matthew 12.27 and Mark 3.27.
[228] Cf. Romans 8.7.
[229] Cf. Proverbs 24.11.
[230] Cf. 1 Corinthians 13.9.
[231] Cf. Romans 1.16.
[232] Cf. Ephesians 1.4.
[233] Galatians 1.20.
[234] Cf. Psalm 70.5.
[235] 2 Timothy 4.7.
[236] Cf. Psalm 69.17.

He repeats his intention to persevere in his mission despite ridicule and insult – presumably from Christian clergy in Britain.

[**45**] So anyone who wants to insult me and laugh at me can do so. But I will not hide, nor be silent[237] about those 'signs and wonders'[238] which were shown to me by the Lord many years before they actually occurred; for he knows everything 'from all eternity'.[239] [**46**] So I should give God thanks without ceasing,[240] for he very often forgave my stupidity[241] and negligence[242] by not being fiercely angry[243] with me who had been appointed his helper.[244] Yet, I was not quick in accepting what he had made clear to me and so 'the Spirit reminded me'.[245] And the Lord 'was merciful' to me 'a thousand, thousand times'[246] because he saw what was within me and that I was ready[247] but that I did not know what I should do about my state [of life]. All the while many were forbidding my mission. Behind my back among themselves they were telling stories and saying: 'Why does this man put himself in danger among enemies "who do not know God"?'[248] I can truly testify that this was not from malice, but because it did not seem right to them that one as rustic as myself

---

[237] Cf. Acts 18.9.
[238] Daniel 3.99; 6.27.
[239] 2 Timothy 1.9.
[240] Cf. 1 Corinthians 1.4.
[241] Cf. Psalm 68.6.
[242] Cf. Psalm 88.8.
[243] 2 Kings 17.18.
[244] Cf. 1 Corinthians 3.9.
[245] John 14.26.
[246] Cf. Exodus 20.6.
[247] Cf. Psalm 118.60.
[248] 2 Thessalonians 1.8.

should do such a thing. But I was not quick to acknowledge the grace that was in me;[249] now, I know what I should have done then.

Patrick's audience has up to this point been those who have doubted him and his mission. Now his attention turns directly to those, wherever they are, who are reading his words. And these readers seem to be first and foremost his converts in Ireland.

[**47**] So now, without any affectation, I have told my brethren and fellow-servants.[250] They believed me because 'I warned and I warn'[251] in order to make your faith more sure and robust.[252] Would indeed that you would imitate greater things and do more powerful things![253] This would be my glory,[254] for 'the wise son is the glory of the father'.[255] [**48**] You all know, as does God, how I lived among you from my youth[256] 'in the faith of truth'[257] 'and with sincerity of heart'.[258] Furthermore, I have acted with good faith towards the nations [i.e. non-Christians] among whom I live, and will continue doing so in the future. 'God knows'[259] 'I have taken advantage of none'[260] of them; and for the

[249] Cf. 1 Timothy 4.14.
[250] This designation uses terms frequently found together in the New Testament, cf. Revelation 6.11.
[251] 2 Corinthians 13.2.
[252] Cf. Job 4.3–4.
[253] This is an echo of the Pauline theme of imitation, cf. the notes on **59**.
[254] Cf. 1 Thessalonians 2.20.
[255] Proverbs 10.1.
[256] Cf. Psalm 70.17.
[257] 2 Thessalonians 2.13.
[258] 1 Corinthians 5.8.
[259] 2 Corinthians 12.2.
[260] 2 Corinthians 12.17; cf. 2 Corinthians 7.2.

sake of God[261] and his Church I would not think of doing so, lest I should provoke persecution[262] of them and of us all, and lest the name of God be blasphemed through me – for it is written: 'Woe to the one through whom the Lord's name is blasphemed.'[263]

In the next few sentences, Patrick appears to be addressing a different set of criticisms, arising in Ireland as to the practicalities of his work. These are challenges against his character – not that he is a sinner and so unworthy, but that his endeavours were motivated by a personal greed for riches. It has given rise to many queries over the years as to social structures within fifth-century Irish society.

[**49**] 'Now even if I am unskilled in everything',[264] yet I have tried in some small way to guard myself for [the sake of] the Christian brethren and the virgins of Christ and 'the religious women'[265] who of their own accord used to give me little gifts. And when they threw any of their ornaments on the altar, I used to return these to them though they were often offended that I should do that. But I did it because of the hope of eternity[266] and so that I could guard myself carefully in everything.[267] Thus,

[261] Cf. 1 Peter 2.13.

[262] Cf. Acts 13.50.

[263] This quotation is a combination of Matthew 18.7 and Romans 2.24. However, Romans 2.24 is the text that Patrick has in mind for it states that 'it is written that "The name of God is blasphemed among the Gentiles because of you"', which is Patrick's exact context; in Paul it is an echo of Isaiah 52.5 and Ezekiel 36.20.

[264] 2 Corinthians 11.6.

[265] Cf. Acts 13.50.

[266] Cf. Wisdom 3.4.

[267] Cf. Ephesians 5.15.

infidels could not, for any reason, catch either me or my ministry of service. And furthermore, by this course of action I did not give unbelievers reason, in even the least matter, to speak against me or to take my character. [50] Maybe when I baptized all those thousands, I hoped to get even half a penny from one of them? 'Tell me and I will return it to you!'[268] Or when the Lord ordained clergy everywhere through me as his mediocre instrument, and I gave my ministry to them for free, did I even charge them the cost of my shoes? 'Tell it against me and I will' all the more 'return it to you!'[269] [51] 'I spend myself'[270] for you that you might lay hold of me.[271] Indeed, I have travelled everywhere for your sake; I have gone amid many dangers, and to places beyond where anyone lived. I have gone where no one else had gone to baptize people, or ordain clergy, or complete people. With God's help, I have carried out all these things lovingly, carefully and most joyfully[272] for your salvation. [52] Sometimes I gave presents to kings – over and above the wages I gave their sons who travelled with me – yet they took me and my companions captive. On that day they avidly sought to kill me, but the time had not yet come.[273] Still they looted us, took everything of value, and bound me in iron. But on the fourteenth day the Lord freed me from their control, and all our

---

[268] 1 Samuel 12.3.

[269] 1 Samuel 12.3.

[270] 2 Corinthians 12.15.

[271] Cf. Matthew 22.15. There is irony here on Patrick's part. The allusion is to those who wished to trap Jesus. Patrick wished himself to be trapped by them so that in this way they might be entrapped by his message.

[272] Cf. 2 Corinthians 12.15.

[273] Cf. John 7.6.

belongings were returned to us for the sake of God[274] and 'the close friends'[275] we had been earlier.

Note the discontinuities in the narrative: those criticizing him seem to be clerics abroad over a personal sin, and at other times Christians or non-Christians in Ireland complaining about money and brides. Sometimes it seems he has left Ireland; at other times he is writing in Ireland; sometimes his ideal reader does not know Ireland; sometimes, as here, they know all the details of his work.

[**53**] You all know well how much I paid those who are judges in all the areas[276] I visited frequently. I suppose I must have paid out the price of fifteen [judges] among them, so that you might enjoy me and I might always enjoy you in God.[277] I am neither sorry about it, nor is it enough for me, so still 'I spend and I will spend all the more'.[278] The Lord is powerful and so he can still grant that 'I might spend' myself 'for your souls'.[279]

[**54**] Behold, 'I call God as the witness in my soul that I do not lie';[280] nor would write in such a way that it would be 'an occasion of greed or false praise';[281] nor do I do so out of a desire for honour from you. Honour which is not yet seen,[282] but which is believed in by the heart[283] is enough for me, 'for he

[274] Cf. 1 Peter 2.13.
[275] Acts 10.24.
[276] This phrase is used on several occasions in Scripture, e.g. Genesis 41.46.
[277] Cf. Romans 15.24.
[278] Cf. 2 Corinthians 12.15.
[279] 2 Corinthians 12.15.
[280] 2 Corinthians 1.23.
[281] Cf. 1 Thessalonians 2.5.
[282] Cf. 2 Corinthians 4.18.
[283] Cf. Romans 10.10.

who promised is faithful'[284] and never lies. [55] Moreover, I see that already 'in this present age'[285] the Lord has highly exalted me. I was not the sort of person [you would expect] the Lord to give this grace to, nor did I deserve it, for I know with the greatest certainty that poverty and woe are more my line than pleasures and riches – after all, Christ the Lord was poor for our sake[286] – and so I too am one who is miserable and unfortunate. Even if I wanted riches, I do not have them 'and I am not judging myself'[287] for not a day passes but I expect to be killed or waylaid or taken into slavery or assaulted in some other way. But for the sake of the promise of heaven 'I fear none of these things'.[288] Indeed, I have cast myself into the hands of God,[289] the almighty one who rules everywhere,[290] as the prophet[291] has said: 'Cast your burden on God, and he will sustain you.'[292]

Now follows a final declaration of Patrick's faith in God: his work, personal identity, and even his life are presented to the Father in the same way as Christ offers all back to the Father in the final discourses and on the cross in John's Gospel. This act of offering oneself brings the whole body of Christ into the perfect glory of which now we have but a glimpse through the life of faith.

[284] Hebrews 10.23.
[285] Galatians 1.4.
[286] Cf. 2 Corinthians 8.9.
[287] 1 Corinthians 4.3.
[288] Acts 20.24.
[289] Cf. Psalm 31.5; Luke 23.46.
[290] 1 Chronicles 29.12.
[291] The designation of the psalmist (David) as a prophet is based on Acts 2.30.
[292] Psalm 54.22.

[**56**] Behold, now 'I commend my spirit' to my 'most faithful God'[293] 'whose ambassador I am'[294] in my unworthiness. However, 'God does not have favourites'[295] and chose me[296] for this task that I might be just one of the least of his servants.[297] [**57**] Therefore, 'I shall give to him for all the things that he has given to me.'[298] But what shall I say to him? What can I promise to give my Lord? I have nothing of value that is not his gift![299] But 'he searches the hearts and the inmost parts'[300] and [knows] that it is enough that I exceedingly desire, and was ready indeed,[301] that he should grant me 'to drink his cup'[302] just as he granted it to others who love him.

[**58**] So may it never happen to me[303] that my God should

---

[293] Cf. Psalm 31.5; Luke 23.46; Acts 7.59; 1 Peter 4.19.

[294] Ephesians 6.20.

[295] Deuteronomy 10.17; cf. Galatians 2.6; 2 Chronicles 19.2; Romans 2.11; Ephesians 6.9; Colossians 3.25.

[296] John 15.16.

[297] Matthew 25.40. Note Patrick's method: a sequence of identifications with Christ and Paul is presented – what they went through, he too is going through; thus he validates his own position and apostolic identity.

[298] Psalm 115.12.

[299] Cf. Wisdom 9.17.

[300] Psalm 6.9; cf. Revelation 2.23. Most translations use some phrase like 'the depths of the soul' for what I have translated as 'inmost parts', but the more graphic nature of the Latin translation should be kept in mind: renes, literally, the kidneys.

[301] Cf. Psalm 118.60.

[302] This use of this gospel phrase is complex. The incident of the disciples proving their devotion by being prepared to drink the same cup as Christ is found in Matthew 20.20–8 and Mark 10.35–41. It is the Marcan account that is most directly relevant for there the two disciples are named and one of them is John – the 'Beloved', cf. John 13.23, etc. As Patrick understands the incident, it means something like this: John says he is ready to drink the Lord's cup, this is granted to him and the other disciple, John is the one who loves and is loved by the Lord. By identifying himself with these disciples, Patrick displays his discipleship, and expects that the cup will be granted. This will be a demonstration of the love between him and the Lord, and will be a promise of his place in the kingdom in heaven.

[303] Cf. 1 Maccabees 13.5.

separate me from his 'people which he has acquired'[304] in the outermost parts of the earth. I pray God that he give me perseverance and deign to grant that I should render him faithful witness until [the moment of] my passing [from this life to the life to come],[305] all for the sake of my God. [**59**] And, if at any time I have 'imitated something that is good'[306] for the sake of my God whom I love, then I ask him to grant me that I may shed my blood[307] 'for his name's sake'[308] with those proselytes and captives, even if this means that I should lack even a tomb,[309] or that my corpse be horribly chopped up by dogs and wild beasts, or that 'the birds of heaven devour it'.[310] I do hereby declare that should this happen to me, I will have gained my soul as well as my body.[311] For should any of these things happen, there is no

[304] Isaiah 43.21.

[305] Patrick views death as a transitus – a move from one sort of life to another. This was a common way of presenting death in both the Fathers and the early Middle Ages; it occurs in contemporary Catholic theology only with reference to the Assumption of Mary.

[306] Cf. 3 John 11. This notion of imitating something good is clearly an echo of this particular text in the New Testament, but it should be remembered that the notion that holiness consists in imitating holiness is a larger theme in early Christian writings, and especially Paul and other writings attributed to him: cf. 1 Corinthians 4.16; 11.1; Ephesians 5.1; Philippians 3.17; 1 Thessalonians 1.6; 2.14; 2 Thessalonians 3.7, 9; Hebrews 6.12; 13.7. As a theme it occurs several times in Patrick, cf. **34**, **42** and **47**.

[307] Cf. Hebrews 12.4.

[308] Links the idea of suffering for the name – Acts 5.41; 9.16 – with that of making converts for the sake of the Lord's name – Romans 1.5.

[309] Cf. Deuteronomy 28.26; Psalm 78.2–3.

[310] Luke 8.5 supplies the wording; but the notion is found in the Old Testament: Jeremiah 7.33; Ezekiel 29.5; and especially in 1 Kings 16.4, and to a lesser degree in 14.11.

[311] There is an echo of two phrases from the Gospel here. First, Matthew 10.28, which raises the possibility of the destruction of the body independently of the soul. Patrick knows that though the body would be destroyed, the soul would not be harmed, and so he is a follower of Christ's words in that he has no fear for his body, but has a fear for his soul. Second, Matthew 16.26 on the value of the soul compared with earthly gain. Patrick presents himself as one who would heed this verse's message: he is prepared to lose the whole world, and gain his soul.

doubt that on the day[312] we shall arise in the brightness of the sun,[313] this is in the glory of Christ Jesus our redeemer,[314] we shall be 'sons of the living God'[315] and 'fellow heirs with Christ'[316] and 'conformed to his image';[317] 'for from him and through him and in him'[318] we shall reign. [**60**] But this sun which we see, rising each day for us by God's command, it shall never reign, nor shall its splendour last.[319] Likewise all those miserable people who worship it shall end up in a foul punishment. We, on the other hand, are those who believe in Christ, and adore him who is the true sun.[320] He is the sun which does not perish, and so we too, 'who do his will,' shall not perish.[321] And, as Christ 'will abide forever'[322] so he [who believes in him] 'will abide forever', for Christ reigns with God the Father almighty, and with the Holy Spirit, before all ages, and now, and 'through all the ages to come'.[323] Amen.

[312] Cf. Ruth 3.13.

[313] Cf. Isaiah 30.26.

[314] Cf. 1 Corinthians 15.43; Philippians 3.20–1.

[315] Romans 8.16; 9.26; cf. Hosea 2.1; cf. also **40**.

[316] Romans 8.17.

[317] Cf. Romans 8.29.

[318] Romans 11.36. This is one of the great doxology phrases and should be seen primarily as a direct echo of the actual liturgy in which Patrick took part, rather than of Paul who is himself echoing liturgy in his use of the phrase in Romans.

[319] Cf. Matthew 5.45. It speaks of God causing the sun to rise on both the righteous and sinners; here Patrick begins with the sun and then described the rewards of both groups.

[320] Christ as 'the sun' or 'the true sun' is a complex theme in early Christian writing which has survived in one or two places in the Latin liturgy even down to modern times. The theme uses a great variety of scriptural passages to develop its mythological coherence such as Matthew 13.43; 17.2; and Revelation 22.5, but these, and other passages like them, should be seen as just elements in a complex development.

[321] Cf. 1 John 2.17.

[322] Cf. Psalm 88.37; 1 John 2.17.

[323] Revelation 11.15.

His signature and farewell

[61] So here it is! I have, again and again, briefly set before you the words of my declaration. 'I bear witness' in truth and joyfulness of heart 'before God and his holy angels'[324] that the one and only purpose I had in going back to that people from whom I had earlier escaped was the gospel and the promises of God.[325]

[62] I now pray for anyone who believes in and fears God[326] who may perchance come upon this writing which Patrick, the sinner and the unlearned one, wrote in Ireland. I wrote it so that no one might say that whatever little I did, or anything I made visible according to God's pleasure, was done through ignorance. Rather, you should judge the situation and let it be truly believed that it was the gift of God. And this is my declaration before I die.

---

[324] 1 Timothy 5.21 (and 2 Timothy 4.1 and Psalm 118.111 from which he derives the phrase to alter the quotation). Patrick no doubt thinks that the moment when he will give this testimony is when the Son of Man comes in the glory of the Father with his holy angels to repay each according to their deeds – cf. Matthew 16.27. See Patrick's *Epistola,* 20.
[325] This is a Pauline theme, cf. Romans 9.4; Galatians 3.21.
[326] Cf. Psalm 65.16.

— Six —

INTRODUCTION TO THE *EPISTOLA*

This short 'letter' plunges us into the world of the fifth century like no other piece of writing from the insular world. Although we can only guess at the specific events that prompted this letter, we know that the fifth century was one of increasing disorder in the West. The withdrawal of the Roman legions from Britain early in the century left a power vacuum of warlords anxious to grab whatever was for the taking, and slaves were an ideal commodity. As the century progressed, raiding, taking captives and holding people for ransom became commonplace not only on the fringes of the Roman world but wherever the new peoples were establishing themselves; for example, among the Franks in Gaul. Patrick knew the whole business intimately as one taken captive himself, and he speaks in this letter from the basis of that experience. Moreover, we should not forget that he is the only person from that period who survived enslavement and told his story.

APOSTATES

This letter seems, on internal evidence, to point to the fact that many who were nominally Christians were also engaging in the practice of raiding and taking captives. Patrick sees this crime as a formal rebellion against God and a rejection of his gift of life so those who are engaged in it are presented as condemned traitors:

apostates. This crime is compounded in that those attacked and enslaved are Christians. The aggressors are killing those with whom they have declared before God, in baptism, that they would be brothers. And there are others who can still be considered Christians who seem to aid these apostates.

In the face of this wickedness, Patrick must issue a formal warning which takes its structure from the parable of the wicked tenants in Matthew 21.33–46/Luke 20.9–16. The wicked soldiers are like the tenants in the parable. They have abandoned the law of God, and have rejected the warnings that have been sent to them. Now judgement is being passed on them by God: their inheritance is to be taken from them.

Patrick is the vehicle by which this judgement is promulgated and anyone who has heard it from him can pass on the news to those reprobate soldiers. Sometimes this is referred to as 'Patrick excommunicating these soldiers', but such expressions are unhelpful as they belong to a canonical system that had not yet developed in the West at the time when this was written. From Patrick's perspective, the wicked soldiers were the ones who passed sentence on themselves. They chose their actions, they rebelled, and Patrick is merely declaring officially what the fruits of those actions are.

MORALITY AND SPIRITUALITY

Two other points are worth noting as they give us an insight into Patrick's understanding of the Christian life. First, Patrick wrote long before the modern distinction between 'moral activity' and 'spirituality'. For Patrick, the aim of the Christian life is to be acceptable as part of the offering of Christ to the Father. The means of communion with this perfect sacrifice of the Son to the Father is by belief in Christ and adherence to a moral code: rejection of either is rebellion. So one must live a life that makes one an offering acceptable in the sight of God. The fact that this part of the Christian life has been ignored by the soldiers of Coroticus calls forth Patrick's most explicit teaching in the form of a simple code of Christian morality.

AUDIENCE

Second, we see the audience Patrick is addressing change many times in the course of this short letter. Sometimes he is addressing the soldiers, sometimes Christians, on one occasion the captives, and once he addresses God in prayer. Clearly, all these audiences cannot be addressed in a single document. So what is the letter? We could see it as a literary form by which Patrick seeks to preach to his own Christian audience, spelling out in detail to them his guidance on the conduct of the Christian's life. In order to bring this home he lets them 'overhear' his words to those whose who have rejected the Christian way, those who are suffering, and his own prayer. Viewed in this way, the letter, far from being a textual and historical conundrum – as it is often perceived – becomes one of the most elegant moral instructions to new converts to Christianity that we possess. It is made all the more poignant in that we can picture the circumstances that prompted it in this period of social upheaval, and we know that Patrick teaches about Christian morality in the face of lawlessness as one who had suffered himself.

Seven

ᏢᎪᎢᎡᏆᏟᏦ'Ꮪꞏ ADDRESS TO THE SOLDIERS OF COROTICUS (The *Epistola*)

Patrick introduces himself and his topic

[1] Patrick, a sinner and one truly unlearned. I declare myself to be a bishop set up by God in Ireland. I most certainly hold that what I am, I have received from God. And so I live as an alien among the barbarians and as a wanderer for the sake of the love of God,[1] as God is my witness. I have not wished to utter anything harshly or roughly: but the zeal of God[2] has forced me, and the truth of Christ[3] raises me up[4] for the love of my neighbours and sons[5] for whom I gave up my homeland and parents, and, if I am worthy, even 'my life up to the grave'.[6] I have sworn to my God to teach the nations,[7] even if some hold me in contempt.

[2] These words, which I have composed and written with 'my own hand',[8] are to be sent, given and proclaimed to the

---

[1] Patrick makes a contrast here between himself and Cain 'the wanderer' of Genesis 4.12; cf. *Confessio* **12**.

[2] Cf. 1 Maccabees 2.54.

[3] Cf. 2 Corinthians 11.10.

[4] Cf. Romans 10.9.

[5] Cf. Sirach 25.2; 2 Corinthians 5.14.

[6] Matthew 26.38; and see Revelation 12.11 for the context.

[7] Cf. Matthew 28.19.

[8] Philemon 19. Writing with one's own hand carries with it a notion of special authority such as that conveyed by Paul at the end of his letters, e.g. 1 Corinthians 16.21.

soldiers of Coroticus. In doing this I do not speak to my compatriots nor to 'fellow-citizens with the' Roman 'saints';[9] but to those who by their evil deeds are servants of the demons. In a hostile manner these allies of the Irish and of the apostate Picts live in death, and are bloodthirsty for the blood of the innocent Christians I have begotten in countless numbers for God and have strengthened in Christ.

Patrick describes the crimes which call forth this letter of judgement upon them. Sending a priest to tell them of their crimes who is then laughed at should not be seen as an example of Patrick's political naïveté. The pattern that Patrick is following is that of the parable of the evil tenants of the vineyard in Matthew 21.33–46/Luke 20.9–16. There, after several warnings, the lord of the vineyard sends his son. It is when the son is not respected – as the owner had expected him to be – but killed, that the moment of judgement comes for those wicked tenants. Patrick sees himself in the place of the owner of the vineyard, and the priest is like his son (hence his insistence that it was not just an ordinary priest he sent to them, but one who was dear to him whom he had instructed since he was an infant). Now with his messenger rejected, the moment has come for the final judgement to be delivered against these evil men.

[3] The day after the anointed neophytes – still wearing their white baptismal garb and with the fragrance of the chrism on their foreheads still about them – were cut down and cruelly put to the sword by these men, I sent to them a holy priest – one I had taught since his infancy – accompanied by other

---

[9] Ephesians 2.19; the text is awkward, but clearly echoes Ephesians.

clerics with a letter. In it I asked them to give back to us the
baptized prisoners that they had taken along with some of the
loot. They treated the whole matter as a big joke.

[4] So now I do not know who to grieve for more:[10] those
who were killed, those captured, or those whom the Devil has
deeply ensnared in his trap.[11] They will be enslaved equally with
him in the everlasting punishment of Gehenna.[12] For it is indeed
true that 'he who commits sin is a slave of sin'[13] and shall be
known as 'a son of the devil'.[14]

*Patrick as judge announces the true spiritual identity of the wicked
soldiers: by their actions they have separated themselves from light and
true life. It is interesting to see how Patrick viewed his ministry: he does
not use images of a representative, but of a plenipotentiary ambassador.
As Patrick sees it, to encounter him is to meet with Christ the judge.*

[5] So let everyone who fears God know[15] that the soldiers of
Coroticus are strangers to me and to Christ, my God, 'for whom
I am an ambassador'.[16] The father-killer and the brother-killer

---

[10] The image is of Patrick grieving before the judgement is carried out and is reminiscent of Christ weeping for Jerusalem – cf. Matthew 23.37.

[11] Cf. Acts 13.10.

[12] James 3.6 – 'Gehenna' is used only here in the Latin Bible.

[13] John 8.34.

[14] Acts 13.10; cf. John 8.44. Note that Patrick sees himself as replacing Paul in Acts
13.8–12: Paul preaches, Paul is opposed, Paul judges, Paul condemns, and then punishment immediately follows.

[15] Cf. Acts 13.16. Patrick appropriates to himself the whole speech – Acts
13.16–47 – for he has been commanded to be a light to the nations and bring salvation
to the ends of the earth – 13.47; cf. Isaiah 49.6.

[16] Ephesians 6.20.

are raging wolves[17] 'eating up' the Lord's 'people like bread'.[18] As it is said: 'The wicked have destroyed your land, O Lord.'[19] For [the Lord] has wonderfully and mercifully planted [his law] in Ireland in these final times;[20] and, with God's help, it has grown there. [**6**] I do not go beyond my authority, for I have a share with those 'whom he called and predestined'[21] to preach the gospel with no small measure of persecutions[22] 'unto the very end of the earth'.[23] So despite the fact that the Enemy[24] begrudges this through the tyranny of Coroticus who fears neither God nor his chosen priests, still it is to these priests that God has granted the highest, the divine and the sublime power: 'those whom they shall bind on earth shall be bound in heaven'.[25]

Patrick now addresses Christians as to how they are to treat the wicked soldiers so as to encourage them to undertake penance as satisfaction for their sins.

[**7**] So I earnestly entreat 'you holy and humble of heart'.[26] It is not lawful to seek favour from men such as these, nor 'to eat

[17] Cf. Acts 20.29; cf. Matthew 7.15; 10.16.
[18] Psalm 13.4; cf. Psalm 52.5.
[19] Psalm 118.126.
[20] Cf. Acts 2.17.
[21] Romans 8.30.
[22] Cf. Mark 10.29–30.
[23] Acts 13.47.
[24] The enemy is the Devil (cf. Acts 13.10 and 1 Peter 5.8).
[25] Matthew 16.19. Note the idea of binding the strong man – Matthew 12.19 – here identified with the Devil, and Patrick's image of the priest as the judge.
[26] Daniel 3.87.

food' or drink 'with them';[27] nor to accept their alms[28] until they make satisfaction to God with painful penance and the shedding of tears;[29] and free the baptized 'servants of God'[30] and the hand-maids of Christ – for whom he was crucified and died.

Patrick sets out a summary of the moral life of Christians. It is only through a life lived in avoiding wickedness and in pursuing virtue that the Christian can approach the Lord.

[**8**] 'The Lord rejects the gifts of the wicked. He who offers a sacrifice from the goods of the poor is as one who sacrifices a son in the sight of his father.'[31] 'The riches' he says 'which he has unjustly gathered will be vomited from his belly; the angel of death will hand him over to be crushed by the anger of dragons; he will be killed with the viper's tongue and an unquenchable fire will consume him.'[32] Hence, 'Woe to him who gathers for himself from the things that are not his.'[33] Or [as it says else-where] 'What does it profit a man if he gains the whole universe and suffers the loss of his soul?'[34]

[**9**] But it would take too long to describe individual crimes and set out the testimonies from the whole law which deal with such greed. [So here are the basics:]

---

[27] 1 Corinthians 5.11.
[28] Cf. Sirach 34.23.
[29] Cf. Psalm 6.6. Patrick is referring to the practice of 'tearful penance'.
[30] 1 Peter 2.16.
[31] Sirach 34.23–4.
[32] Job 20.15, 16, 26.
[33] Habakkuk 2.6.
[34] Matthew 16.26.

- Avarice is a deadly crime;[35]
- 'You shall not covet your neighbour's goods';[36]
- 'You shall not kill';[37]
- A murderer cannot be with Christ;[38]
- 'He who hates his brother is a murderer';[39] or
- 'He who does not love his brother remains in death'.[40]

So how much more guilty is the man who stains his hands with the blood of 'the sons of God'[41] whom [God] has acquired recently in the very ends of the earth[42] through the preaching of us who are so insignificant?

The tone changes considerably in the next section of the letter. Patrick thinks of how people react to him and defends his credentials and his activity in Ireland. This part of the letter closely resembles the Confessio *in its defensiveness of his integrity combined with his assertiveness of his position.*

[10] Was it without God, or 'according to the flesh'[43] that I came to Ireland? Who forced me to come? 'I am one bound in the

---

[35] This is the only item on his list of basic moral rules that is not taken directly from Scripture, but it clearly echoes statements about greed such as Luke 12.15.

[36] Exodus 20.17. This gathering of crimes is found in Romans 13.9 and is based on the decalogue.

[37] Exodus 20.13.

[38] Cf. 1 Peter 4.15.

[39] 1 John 3.15.

[40] 1 John 3.14.

[41] Cf. Galatians 3.26.

[42] Cf. Isaiah 41.9. Note it invokes the idea found elsewhere in Patrick's writings that he works at 'the ends of the earth'.

[43] 1 Corinthians 1.17.

Spirit'[44] so that I cannot see any of my relatives. Is it from within me that the holy mercy arises which I show towards this people – a people who once took me prisoner and destroyed the servants, male and female, of my father's estate? I was a free man 'according to the flesh',[45] my father a *decurion*, and I sold my status for the benefit of others. I am neither ashamed of this nor sorry, but thus I have arrived at this point: I am a servant in Christ to a foreign people for the ineffable glory 'of the eternal life which is in Christ Jesus our Lord',[46] [11] even though my own people do not know me, for 'a prophet has no honour in his own country'.[47]

In the face of the crimes that are committed, and in response to the charges that are being voiced by one group against another, Patrick replies by appealing to the unity of the Church: it is one fold as it has one shepherd, one Lord, one God. Jesus Christ is the source of unity and calls his people to share in his work. In this all – Picts, Irish and Romans – must take part, recognizing that the Lord's call is greater than any one of them.

Perhaps we are not from 'the one fold'[48] nor have we 'one God and Father',[49] as he says: 'He that is not with me is against me; and he who does not gather with me, scatters.'[50] It is not right

---

[44] Acts 20.22.
[45] 1 Corinthians 1.17.
[46] Romans 6.23.
[47] John 4.44.
[48] John 10.16.
[49] Ephesians 4.6.
[50] Matthew 12.30.

that 'one destroys, another builds'.[51] 'I am not seeking my own way',[52] for it is not from me but from God's grace 'who put this care in my heart'[53] that I should be one of the hunters and fishers[54] whom long ago he foretold would come 'in the last days'.[55]

The next section is not a return to the theme of self-defence against criticisms. Rather Patrick addresses God, asking what should happen now since the wicked soldiers do not listen to his preaching.

[**12**] They despise me. Oh, how they look down on me! O Lord, what am I to do? Behold around me are your sheep torn to pieces and afflicted by those robbers[56] under the command of the bad-minded Coroticus. Far from the love of God is the man who hands over Christians into the hands of the Irish and the Picts. 'Fierce wolves' have devoured the flock[57] of the Lord which with the greatest love and care[58] was truly increasing beautifully in Ireland. Indeed, I could not count how many of the sons and daughters of the rulers of the Irish had become monks and virgins of Christ. On account of this, 'Do not be pleased with the wrong done by the unjust, knowing that even unto depths of hell it shall not please the wicked.'[59]

[51] Sirach 34.28.
[52] Cf. 1 Corinthians 13.5.
[53] 2 Corinthians 8.16.
[54] Cf. Jeremiah 16.16.
[55] Acts 2.17.
[56] Cf. John 10.8–12.
[57] Acts 20.29; cf. Matthew 7.15.
[58] Cf. John 21.15.
[59] Sirach 9.17. This verse cannot now be found in translations of the Scriptures as it belongs to the so-called 'Expanded Text' which stands behind the Vetus Latina/Vulgate. It can be conveniently found only in editions of the Vulgate or older Catholic translations such as the Douay.

Patrick now addresses his fellow-Christians once again to upbraid them that they collude, if not collaborate, with those who are committing crimes. He seems to be advocating a policy of paying ransoms for some of those taken captive. He cites the example of Gaul where we know that bishops such as St Caesarius of Arles did pay ransoms to the invading barbarians to get back Christian captives.

[**13**] Which of the saints would not be horrified at the prospect of fun, parties or enjoyment with the likes of these men? They have filled their homes with plunder taken from dead Christians and they live by this. Wretched men! They do not know the poisonous lethal food that they share with their children and friends. They are like Eve who did not understand that in reality she gave death 'to her husband'.[60] All who do evil are like this, they work towards the everlasting penalty of death.[61]

[**14**] This is the practice of the Roman Christians of Gaul. They send suitable holy men to the Franks and other pagan peoples with great piles of money to buy back baptized captives. You, however, kill them and sell them to a foreign 'nation which does not know God'.[62] You are like someone who hands over 'the members of Christ' to a brothel.[63] Do you have any 'hope in God'?[64] Who can approve of you? Who can address you with any words of praise? God will judge – as it is written: 'Not only those who do evil, but those also who approve of it, will be damned.'[65]

[60] Genesis 3.6.
[61] Cf. 2 Corinthians 7.10.
[62] 1 Thessalonians 4.5.
[63] 1 Corinthians 6.15.
[64] Acts 24.15.
[65] Romans 1.32.

Patrick expresses his grief over the sufferings of those taken captive.

[15] I do not know 'what' more 'to say or how to speak'[66] about these dead 'sons of God'[67] whom the sword struck so harshly. Indeed, it is written: 'Weep with those who weep';[68] and in another place: 'If one member suffers, all the members suffer with it.'[69] This is the reason why the Church suffers and mourns for its sons and daughters[70] who have not yet been put to the sword, but who were carried off and brought to distant lands where sin abounds openly,[71] grievously and without shame. There freeborn men are offered for sale and Christians are made into slaves again,[72] indeed slaves of the worst and most unworthy of men: the apostate Picts.

[16] So with sadness and grief I cry out: O 'most beloved' and radiant brothers and 'sons' – you are more than I can count – to whom I 'have given birth in Christ'.[73] What shall I do with you, I who am not worthy to come to the assistance of God or men? 'The wickedness of the unjust has prevailed over us.'[74] We have

[66] John 12.49.

[67] This phrase is used on four occasions in the New Testament – Matthew 5.9; Luke 20.36; Romans 8.14, 19; Galatians 3.26 – but since Patrick seems to have the argument from Romans in his mind, it probably reflects Paul's usage there, where the sons of God are those who have been delivered from slavery by Christ but who have to put up with sufferings in the present life as they await the full revelation of glory at the end.

[68] Romans 12.15.

[69] 1 Corinthians 12.26.

[70] Cf. Matthew 2.18.

[71] Cf. Romans 5.20.

[72] Patrick echoes the theme of Romans 8. The Christians are those delivered from slavery, and they must not fall back in fear and slavery – Romans 8.15 – so Patrick is not only concerned that they are physically the prisoners of the Picts and made into slaves, but also that being with these sinful men, they might fall back into a former spiritual slavery.

[73] Cf. 1 Corinthians 4.14–15.

[74] Cf. Psalm 64.4.

become like strangers. Perhaps they do not believe that we have received 'one baptism' and have 'one God and Father'?[75] That we are from Ireland is an unworthy thing to them. As [Scripture] says: 'Do you not have one God? Why do each of you abandon your neighbour?'[76]

[17] And so my dearest friends, I grieve, grieve deeply, for you, but at the same time I rejoice within myself: 'I did not labour in vain'[77] and my journeying has not been useless. For while such an indescribably awful crime has occurred, still, thanks be to God, it is as faithful baptized people that you have left this world to go to Paradise.[78] I can see you. You have not begun your migration to where 'there is no night, nor sorrow, and where death shall be no more'[79] and 'You shall rejoice leaping like calves let loose from their stalls. And you shall tread down the wicked, for they will be ashes under the soles of your feet.'[80] [18] And then you will reign with the apostles, prophets and martyrs and take possession of an eternal kingdom. Of this he himself testifies when he says: 'They will come from east and west and sit at table with Abraham, Isaac, and Jacob in the kingdom of the heavens.'[81] 'Outside are the dogs and sorcerers and murderers'[82] and 'liars and perjurers, their lot shall be in the

[75] Cf. Ephesians 4.5–6.
[76] Malachi 2.10.
[77] Philippians 2.16.
[78] Cf. Luke 23.43.
[79] This is a conflation of Revelation 22.5 and 21.4.
[80] Malachi 4.2–3.
[81] Matthew 8.11.
[82] Revelation 22.15. Patrick intends the whole verse to be understood: 'Outside are the dogs and sorcerers and fornicators and murderers and idolaters, and everyone who loves and practises falsehood.'

lake of everlasting fire'.[83] It is not without good reason that the apostle says: 'If the just man is barely saved, where will the sinner and the impious transgressor of the law appear?'[84]

Having described the victory and reward to which the saints can look forward in heaven, Patrick now offers the contrast of the reward to be reaped by the soldiers of Coroticus. By their actions they have abandoned morality, and in so doing they have abandoned God. So they are cut off as apostates from the source from which they should be drawing life.

[**19**] What then is the case with Coroticus and his criminal band? Where will these rebels against Christ appear? They are the ones who distribute baptized young women as prizes and all for the sake of a wretched temporal kingdom which will vanish[85] 'in a moment'[86] like a cloud,[87] or indeed 'like smoke scattered by the wind'.[88] 'So the' lying 'sinner will perish from before the face of the Lord, but the just will feast'[89] in great harmony with Christ. 'They will judge the nations and rule'[90] over wicked kings for ever and ever.[91] Amen.

---

[83] Revelation 21.8: 'But as for the cowardly, the faithless, the polluted, as for murderers, fornicators, sorcerers, idolaters, and all liars, their lot shall be in the lake that burns with fire and sulphur, which is the second death.' This conflation is a product of Patrick's memory. Items in one list triggering a combination with a similar list. See also Malachi 3.5 and 1 Timothy 1.10.

[84] 1 Peter 4.18; cf. Proverbs 11.31.

[85] Cf. Luke 12.33–4.

[86] 1 Corinthians 15.52.

[87] Cf. Isaiah 44.22.

[88] Cf. Wisdom 5.15.

[89] Psalm 68.2–3.

[90] Wisdom 3.8.

[91] Cf. Revelation 20.10; 22.5.

As God's representative, Patrick promulgates a public warning to the soldiers of the dire consequences of their actions. Note how Patrick uses the forensic tone: you now stand warned!

[20] 'I testify before God and his angels'[92] that it will come about just as he has indicated by one as unlearned as myself. These are not my words but words which never lie: those of God and 'his apostles and prophets'.[93] I am but the one who has announced them in Latin. 'He that believes will be saved, he who does not believe will be condemned.'[94] 'God has spoken.'[95]

[21] I earnestly request that any servant of God who is capable of bringing these tidings to public notice should do so: let such a messenger neither hide nor detract from them but read them aloud so that every person, and Coroticus himself, should hear them. If this happens then God may inspire them, and they may return to him.[96] For though it be very late, it may be they will repent of their impious actions – being the murderers of the Lord's brothers and sisters – and release the baptized captives they have taken. Thus they would merit to live[97] in God and be healed for this life and eternity.

Peace in the Father and the Son and the Holy Spirit. Amen.

[92] 1 Timothy 5.21; 2 Timothy 4.1. See the *Confessio*, **61**.

[93] Ephesians 3.5.

[94] Mark 16.15–16.

[95] This phrase is used on many occasions in Scripture. Those at Psalm 59.8 and Psalm 107.8 are particularly interesting.

[96] Cf. 2 Timothy 2.25–6.

[97] Cf. Acts 28.4.

FURTHER READING

The quantity of literature devoted to Patrick is vast. There are several editions of his works in Latin, numerous translations, and the number of books, chapters and articles about him runs into several thousands. What is given here is only a preliminary reading list intended primarily to provide more background to the text of Patrick as well as identify those works which are mentioned in other places in this book. However, it also provides a basis from which someone can embark on a more detailed and extensive study of Patrick. See the last section of this chapter for an alphabetical list of works cited and publishing details.

EDITIONS OF PATRICK IN LATIN

There are two important Latin editions of Patrick. The first is N. J. D. White, 'Libri Sancti Patricii: The Latin Writings of St Patrick' 1905. This text with a minimal apparatus was available as a pamphlet with the same title from SPCK, London in 1918. White has been used as the basis of this translation; however, many scholars have relied solely on the edition of L. Bieler, *Libri Epistolarum Sancti Patricii Episcopi*, 1952. I have consulted it throughout this translation, bearing in mind the reservations of M. Esposito, 'St Patrick's "Confessio" and the "Book of Armagh"', 1954.

CONCORDANCE

There is a concordance to the Latin text of Patrick's works by K. Devine, *A Computer-Generated Concordance to the Libri Epistolarum of Saint Patrick (Clauis Patricii I)*, 1989.

TRANSLATIONS

There have been many translations, some providing a parallel Latin text, and almost all providing some background to Patrick. Both White and Bieler produced English translations; White as *The Writings of St Patrick: His Life and*

Writings, 1920 (with many reprints under slightly different titles); and Bieler in *The Works of St Patrick and St Secundinus: Hymn on St Patrick*, 1953. A typical translation is that of A. B. E. Hood, *St Patrick: His Writings and Muirchú's Life*, 1978. It is the work of a historian, and the emphasis in the notes is on locating Patrick against what we know of the fifth century.

The works of R. P. C. Hanson, *The Life and Writings of the Historical Saint Patrick*, 1983, and D. Conneely, *The Letters of Saint Patrick*, 1993, are similar as they are both keenly interested in locating Patrick against the background of Latin patristic thought. Conneely's work attempts to find echoes of the Latin fathers in his work, but the links found are often tenuous. The book reprints Bieler's text with an English translation by Thomas Finan. As works seeking to locate Patrick in his theological culture, Hanson and Conneely share a common weakness: both want to view him against the backdrop of the major Latin fathers (especially Augustine), while they fail to situate him in his own context of the theological culture of fifth-century Gaul.

Another recent study is that of D. Howlett, *The Book of Letters of Saint Patrick the Bishop*, 1994. Howlett's thesis is that there is a profound biblical style underlying the seemingly rustic Latin of Patrick.

Lastly, in a collection of many texts connected with Patrick and early Christian Ireland entitled *Saint Patrick's World*, 1993, L. de Paor has provided a translation of Patrick. Anyone wishing to study the sources relating to Patrick from the fifth century and later, but who does not wish to pursue the Latin originals, would do well to start with this convenient source book.

HISTORICAL CONTEXT

For a general background to Patrick and early Christian Ireland, the following works deserve special mention: K. Hughes, *The Church in Early Irish Society*, 1966; chs 1–4 and 11 deal with Patrick and the reuse of Patrick; and D. Ó Cróinín, *Early Medieval Ireland: 400–1200*, 1995; the early chapters of this general history of early medieval Ireland deal with Patrick and the earliest historical evidence.

For a detailed window into everyday life, and an introduction to the structure of early Irish society, F. Kelly, *Early Irish Farming*, 1997, is indispensable.

The Celtic culture of Ireland, and its pre-Christian religion, have been the subjects of a vast number of studies in recent years. However, the scholarly worth of much of this writing is open to doubt; some of it is simply nostalgia and romanticism, some of it part of an attempt to promote a contemporary religious eclecticism. In the midst of this noise there are two works which combine accessibility with sound scholarship. The first, presenting what we know of pre-Christian Celtic religion, is S. Piggott, *The Druids*, 1968; the other presenting an overview of Celtic society in Ireland prior to Patrick is B. Raftery, *Pagan Celtic Ireland*, 1994. Most works which present details of Celtic religion depend heavily on one important article: J. J. Tierney, 'The Celtic Ethnography of Posidonius', *Proceedings of the Royal Irish Academy* 60c, pp. 189–275, 1959–60.

SPECIALIZED STUDIES OF PATRICK

Detailed studies of Patrick are too numerous to mention. Some attempt an overall assessment, others deal with specific questions such as where he might have been born, and some with points of detail in Patrick's writings. This selection is more illustrative of the range of material than an attempt to pick out the more significant studies. They are arranged here in chronological order of publication.

J. B. Bury, *The Life of St Patrick and His Place in History*, 1905.

E. MacNeill, 'The Native Place of St Patrick', 1926.

M. Esposito, 'Notes on Latin Learning and Literature in Medieval Ireland: part V, ii, Latin Lives of St Patrick', 1937.

J. A. Ryan, 'A Difficult Phrase in the "Confession" of St Patrick', 1938.

T. F. O'Rahilly, *The Two Patricks: A Lecture on the History of Christianity in Fifth-Century Ireland*, 1942.

L. Bieler, 'The "Creeds" of St Victorinus and St Patrick', 1948.

L. Bieler, *The Life and Legend of Saint Patrick*, 1949.

L. Bieler, 'The Place of St Patrick in Latin Language and Literature', 1952.

L. Bieler, 'St Patrick: A Native of Anglesea?', 1953.

C. Mohrmann, *The Latin of Saint Patrick*, 1961.

J. Carney, *The Problem of St Patrick*, 1961.

D. A. Binchy, 'Patrick and His Biographers, Ancient and Modern', 1962.

F. Shaw, 'Post-Mortem on the Second Patrick', 1963.

L. Bieler, 'The Book of Armagh' in *The Great Books of Ireland: Thomas Davis Lectures March 1964*, 1967.

R. P. C. Hanson, *Saint Patrick: His Origins and Career*, 1968.

D. A. Binchy, 'St Patrick's First Synod', *Studia Hibernica*, 1968.

R. P. C. Hanson, 'The Omissions in the Text of the Confession of St Patrick in the Book of Armagh', 1975.

A. Gwynn, 'The Problem of the *Dicta Patricii*', 1975–6.

P. Dronke, 'St Patrick's Reading', 1981.

R. P. C. Hanson, 'Witness from St Patrick to the Creed of 381', 1983.

J. F. Kelly, 'The Escape of Saint Patrick from Ireland', 1985.

N. D. O'Donoghue, *Aristocracy of Soul: Patrick of Ireland*, 1987.

R. P.C. Hanson, 'The Mission of St Patrick', 1989.

D. N. Dumville, *Saint Patrick AD 493–1993*, 1993.

J. Higgins, 'Two Passages in the *Confessio* of Patrick', 1995.

R. Keogh, 'St Patrick's Escape: Lies or Statistics?', 1997.

The Patrick Legend

Anyone wishing to study Patrick must also come to grips with his medieval hagiographers, primarily Muirchú, but also the later writers and the cult of Patrick in general. The standard edition of Muirchú, with a translation, is by L. Bieler, *The Patrician Texts in the Book of Armagh*, 1979. There are also translations by A. B. E. Hood and L. de Paor accompanying their translations of Patrick's own writings. Other texts and translations include: K. Mulchrone, *Bethu Phátraic: The Tripartite Life of Patrick*, 1939; L. Bieler, *Four Latin Lives of Saint Patrick*, 1971; and F. J. Byrne and P. Francis, 'Two Lives of Saint Patrick: Vita Secunda et Quarta', 1994.

Studies of these lives include:

L. Bieler, 'Studies on the Text of Muirchú', 1950.

L. Bieler, 'The Hymn of St Secundinus', 1953.

L. Bieler, 'Muirchú's Life of Patrick as a Work of Literature', 1974.

L. Bieler, 'Hagiography and Romance in Medieval Ireland', 1975.

T. O'Loughlin, 'St Patrick and an Irish Theology', 1994.

T. O'Loughlin, 'Muirchú's Vita Patricii: A Note on an Unidentified Source', 1996.

For an introduction to the literary genre of hagiography, the best guide is H. Delehaye, *The Legends of the Saints* (the most recent edition, with an introduction by T. O'Loughlin pointing out problems in Irish hagiography, is Dublin, 1998). L. Bieler picked up some specific problems relating to Patrick's legend in 'The Celtic Hagiographer', 1962.

Still Further Reading

Those who wish to build a full bibliography of Patrick should consult these specialist bibliographical guides:

J. F. Kenney, *The Sources for the Early History of Ireland: Ecclesiastical*, 1929, pp. 165–70.

E. Coccia, 'La cultura irlandese precarolingia: Miracolo o mito?', 1967.

M. Lapidge and R. Sharpe, *A Bibliography of Celtic Latin Literature*, 1985, nn. 25–6, 301, 303, 354–60, 365–8, 375, 1,021 and 1,184.

A. Harvey, *Clauis Patricii III: An Annotated Bibliography of St Patrick*, forth-coming.

INDEX OF FURTHER READING

The following arranges in alphabetical order of author all the works referred to in the preceding sections of this chapter.

Bieler, L., 'The Book of Armagh' in *The Great Books of Ireland: Thomas Davis Lectures March 1964*, pp. 51–63, Dublin: Mercier Press 1967.

Bieler, L., 'The Celtic Hagiographer', *Studia Patristica*, 5, pp. 243–65, 1962.

Bieler, L., 'The "Creeds" of St Victorinus and St Patrick', *Theological Studies*, 9, pp. 121–4, 1948.

Bieler, L., *Four Latin Lives of Saint Patrick*, Dublin: Dublin Institute for Advanced Studies 1971.

Bieler, L., 'Hagiography and Romance in Medieval Ireland', *Medievalia et humanistica*, 6, pp. 13–24, 1975.

Bieler, L., 'The Hymn of St Secundinus', *Proceedings of the Royal Irish Academy*, 55c, pp. 117–27, 1955.

Bieler, L., *Libri Epistolarum Sancti Patricii Episcopi*, Dublin: Irish Manuscripts Commission 1952.

Bieler, L., *The Life and Legend of Saint Patrick*, Dublin: Brown & Nolan 1949.

Bieler, L., 'Muirchú's Life of Patrick as a Work of Literature', *Medium Aevum*, 43, pp. 219–33, 1974.

Bieler, L., *The Patrician Texts in the Book of Armagh*, Dublin: Dublin Institute for Advanced Studies 1979.

Bieler, L., 'The Place of St Patrick in Latin Language and Literature', *Vigiliae Christianae*, 6, pp. 65–98, 1952.

Bieler, L., 'St Patrick: A Native of Anglesea?', *Éigse*, 7, pp. 129–31, 1953.

Bieler, L., 'Studies on the Text of Muirchú', *Proceedings of the Royal Irish Academy*, 52c, pp. 179–220, 1950.

Bieler, L., *The Works of St Patrick and St Secundinus: Hymn on St Patrick*, Ancient Christian Writers 17, Washington: Newman Press 1953.

Binchy, D. A., 'Patrick and His Biographers, Ancient and Modern', *Studia Hibernica*, 2, pp. 7–173, 1962.

Binchy, D. A., 'St Patrick's First Synod', *Studia Hibernica*, 8, pp. 49–59, 1968.

Bury, J. B., *The Life of St Patrick and His Place in History*, London: Macmillan 1905.

Byrne, F. J., and Francis, P., 'Two Lives of Saint Patrick: Vita Secunda et Quarta', *Journal of the Royal Society of Antiquaries of Ireland*, 124, pp. 5–117, 1994.

Carney, J., *The Problem of St Patrick*, Dublin: Dublin Institute of Advanced Studies 1961.

Coccia, E., 'La cultura irlandese precarolingia: Miracolo o mito?' *Studi Medievali*, 8, pp. 272–4 [Patrick], 366–70 [Patrician hagiography], 1967.

Conneely, D., *The Letters of Saint Patrick*, Maynooth: An Sagart 1993.

Cróinín, D. Ó., *Early Medieval Ireland: 400–1200*, Dublin: Longmans 1995.

Delehaye, D., *The Legends of the Saints*, Dublin: Four Courts Press 1998.

Devine, K., *A Computer-Generated Concordance to the Libri Epistolarum of Saint Patrick (Clauis Patricii I)*, Dublin: Royal Irish Academy 1989.

Dronke, P., 'St Patrick's Reading', *Cambridge Medieval Celtic Studies*, 1, pp. 31–8, 1981.

Dumville, D. N., *St Patrick AD 493–1993*, Woodbridge: Boydell & Brewer 1993.

Esposito, M., 'Notes on Latin Learning and Literature in Medieval Ireland: part V, ii, Latin Lives of St Patrick', *Hermathena*, 50, pp. 139–44, 1937.

Esposito, M., 'St Patrick's "Confessio" and the "Book of Armagh"', *Irish Historical Studies*, 8, pp. 1–12, 1954.

Gwynn, A., 'The Problem of the *Dicta Patricii*', *Seanchas Ard Mhacha*, 8, pp. 69–80, 1975–6.

Hanson, R. P. C., *The Life and Writings of the Historical Saint Patrick*, New York: Phillimore 1983.

Hanson, R. P.C., 'The Mission of St Patrick', in Mackey, J., ed., *An Introduction to Celtic Christianity*, pp. 22–44, Edinburgh: T. & T. Clark 1989.

Hanson, R. P.C., 'The Omissions in the Text of the Confession of St Patrick in the Book of Armagh', *Studia Patristica*, 12, pp. 91–5, 1975.

Hanson, R. P.C., *Saint Patrick: His Origins and Career*, Oxford: Clarendon 1968.

Hanson, R. P.C., 'Witness from St Patrick to the Creed of 381', *Analecta Bollandiana*, 101, pp. 297–9, 1983.

Harvey, A., *Clauis Patricii III: An Annotated Bibliography of St Patrick*, DMLCS Ancillary Publication 6, Dublin: Royal Irish Academy, forthcoming.

Higgins, J., 'Two Passages in the *Confessio* of Patrick', *Milltown Studies*, 35, pp. 130–3, 1995.

Hood, A. B. E., *St Patrick: His Writings and Muirchú's Life*, Chichester: Seabury Press 1978.

Howlett, D., *The Book of Letters of Saint Patrick the Bishop*, Dublin: Four Courts Press 1994.

Hughes, K., *The Church in Early Irish Society*, London: Methuen 1966.

Kelly, F., *Early Irish Farming*, Dublin: Dublin Institute for Advanced Studies 1997.

Kelly, J. F., 'The Escape of Saint Patrick from Ireland', *Studia Patristica*, 18, pp. 41–5, 1985.

Kenney, J. F., *The Sources for the Early History of Ireland: Ecclesiastical*, New York: Columbia University Press 1929.

Keogh, R., 'St Patrick's Escape: Lies or Statistics?' *History Ireland*, 5, 1, pp. 25–7, 1997.

Lapidge, M. and Sharpe, R., *A Bibliography of Celtic Latin Literature*, Dublin: Royal Irish Academy 1985.

MacNeill, E., 'The Native Place of St Patrick', *Proceedings of the Royal Irish Academy*, 37c, pp. 118–40, 1926.

Mohrmann, C., *The Latin of Saint Patrick*, Dublin: Dublin Institute for Advanced Studies 1961.

Mulchrone, K., *Bethu Phátraic: The Tripartite Life of Patrick*, Dublin: Brown & Nolan 1939.

O'Donoghue, N. D., *Aristocracy of Soul: Patrick of Ireland*, London: Darton, Longman and Todd 1987.

O'Loughlin, T., 'St Patrick and an Irish Theology', *Doctrine and Life*, 44, pp. 153–9, 1994.

O'Loughlin, T., 'Muirchú's Vita Patricii: A Note on an Unidentified Source', *Ériu*, 46, pp. 89–93, 1996.

O'Rahilly, T. F., *The Two Patricks: A Lecture on the History of Christianity in Fifth-Century Ireland*, Dublin: Dublin Institute for Advanced Studies 1942.

de Paor, L., *Saint Patrick's World*, Dublin: Four Courts Press 1993.

Piggott, S., *The Druids*, London: Thames & Hudson 1968.

Raftery, B., *Pagan Celtic Ireland*, London: Thames & Hudson 1994.

Ryan, J. A., 'A Difficult Phrase in the "Confession" of St Patrick', *Irish Ecclesiastical Record*, 52, pp. 293–9, 1938.

Shaw, F., 'Post-Mortem on the Second Patrick', *Studies*, 51, pp. 237–67, 1963.

Tierney, J. J., 'The Celtic Ethnography of Posidonius', *Proceedings of the Royal Irish Academy*, 60c, pp. 189–275, 1959–60.

White, N. J. D., 'Libri Sancti Patricii: The Latin Writings of St Patrick', *Proceedings of the Royal Irish Academy*, 25c, pp. 201–362, 1905.

White, N. J. D., *Libri Sancti Patricii: The Latin Writings of St Patrick*, London: SPCK 1918.

White, N. J. D., *The Writings of St Patrick: His Life and Writings*, London: SPCK 1920.

INDEX OF PATRICK'S USE OF SCRIPTURE

The number beside each biblical reference refers to the standard section numbers used for identification of passages in Patrick's *Confessio* (C) and *Epistola* (E). No distinction is made here between explicit and implicit quotations, nor between allusions and echoes, as this is made clear in the notes, and it is frequently unclear when Patrick is consciously invoking Scripture and when he is simply using familiar biblical phrases. Such judgements would require a detailed study, and it would be inappropriate to preclude such a study in this index.

30562803R00072

Printed in Great Britain
by Amazon